THE GREAT AWAKENING

A Christian Guide To Using Cryptocurrencies For Creating A Private, Prosperous And Free Life Outside The Mark Of The Beast System

D.D. DWASE

****All Scripture Quotations are from the King James Version of the Bible (KJV), unless otherwise stated.*

To every child of God, a dreamer, a champion; to every heart yearning for progress and helping to build a new world, fuelled by ambition and compassion, where dreams take flight, thrive & prosper.

"Ye shall not fear them: for the Lord your God He shall fight for you".

~ Deuteronomy 3:22

THE GREAT AWAKENING

A Christian Guide To Using
Cryptocurrencies For Creating A Private,
Prosperous And Free Life Outside The
Mark Of The Beast System

Contents

Freedom Is The Greater Good   12

CHAPTER 1
The Awakened Path To Enlightenment   20

CHAPTER 2
The Greatest Threat To Our Liberty, Privacy And
Future Prosperity   48

CHAPTER 3
BIS: The Private Organisation Enslaving Humanity   64

CHAPTER 4
The Banking Contagion: Why European & US
Banks Are Deliberately Been Destroyed To Usher
In CBDCs   82

CHAPTER 5
Why Cryptocurrencies Are A Threat To The
Current Financial System And The Way Money
Is Handled   122

CHAPTER 6
A New Kind Of Freedom: Why Private
Cryptocurrencies Is Our Rebellion   146

CHAPTER 7
Be The Wise Servant   172

CHAPTER 8
Rising Above Adversity And Overcoming
Challenges With Resilience   **184**

CHAPTER 9
Cultivating A Victorious Spirit   **204**

CHAPTER 10
Getting Closer To The End-Times   **212**

You Are Priceless   **226**

Other Books By The Author   **232**

About The Author   **246**

THE GREAT AWAKENING

Freedom Is The Greater Good

If you give them an inch, they'll take a mile. But they will take that mile inch by inch so that you don't notice. Every crisis will be another excuse for taking one more inch of your freedom.

Everyone is getting so outraged all the time, constantly offended and distressed at the state of the world. Yes, it's been very exhausting and tiring to watch this all unfold but at the same time it's a special honour to be alive right now. In my opinion, you're watching a scripted movie designed by God to awaken the masses.

But as for you, ye thought evil against me; but God meant it unto good, to bring to pass, as it is this day, to save much people alive.

Genesis 50:20

The Great Awakening & Unveiling Like Never Before

That doesn't mean that we don't participate in enacting change, far from it. But it does give us a steady belief that there's nothing that can stop what is coming. That faith is an anchor of the great awakening in these trying times. If you don't have it, you're going to constantly feel weary, disheartened and troubled when perhaps you're not supposed to hold that entire burden.

While the central banksters move forward with their plans for total surveillance over everyone and everything in society, total control over your money, and total power over your life, there's a huge *"Great Awakening"* happening with people moving forward with plans for maximum privacy in their personal and economic lives, decentralized control over their money, and the power to live prosperously in peace and freedom.

Against A Financial Iceberg

The economy and the financial system are like the Titanic. Most people on the Titanic are painfully unaware of how serious things are about to get. And they have no idea that those steering the Titanic are the very central bankers attempting to upend and destroy everything they loved about the current system. Because for all its faults, at least fiat cash still allows for some level of privacy, security, and anonymity.

However, the central bankers are tearing that away from the people. They're steering the economy right into a gigantic, terrifying financial CBDC (central bank digital currency) iceberg. The CBDC iceberg will crack open and destroy the economy in ways most people can't begin to understand.

And everyone stuck on the Titanic will be swallowed by the cold, cruel waters of the technocratic mark of the beast CBDC financial system. Freedom of speech, the right to privacy, and so many more liberties will be absolutely lost if you do nothing at this pivotal moment in history. Money will cease to be money. You won't own it ever again. You will have literally ZERO control over it.

CBDCs will simply grant you the "privilege" of using the central bank's money, but that privilege can be revoked at any time. You're on the precipice of a financial life-or-death scenario. But the "awakened" can see the CBDC Iceberg ahead. And I've been shouting at the top of my lungs warning people about it. The ***"Great Awakening"*** is a lifeboat created to carry you away to safety from the incoming financial crash.

It will ferry you to a secure island where you can have your freedom, your privacy, your security, and build a life of prosperity outside of the CBDC financial beast system. It will be a little oasis of freedom surrounded by the choppy waters of tyranny. You don't have to feed the beast system. Or give up total

control to the government. Or be tracked
and traced at all times.

Awakened Over Two Decades Preparing For The Coming Mark of The Beast Financial Surveillance System

I have being awakened and worked for
peace and freedom for over two decades
and when I heard about cryptocurrencies
for the first time in 2010, I knew it was
going to change a lot of things. Since
then, I've spent countless hours learning
and mastering this new technology, and
I've helped many people get started with
crypto. I strongly believe that
cryptocurrencies and decentralised
technology can free you from financial
tyranny and monetary manipulation. I'm

determined to help other people take advantage of the benefits of cryptocurrencies that can change their lives. In this book you'll discover how to own a piece of the most disruptive technology since the internet, how to build a total financial system and eventually a parallel society totally independent from the central banker-controlled mark of the beast financial system.

You can build wealth for the future without it being seized. You'll be able to buy and sell goods and services without worrying about them being monitored or shut down. You can establish local trade networks, barter systems and parallel marketplaces. And you can form whole communities of like-minded people to

support each other without depending on
the CBDC control grid.

Are you ready to have your freedom,
your privacy, and your security and build
a life of prosperity outside of the CBDC
mark of the beast financial system?

CHAPTER 1

The Awakened Path
To Enlightenment

As a child of God, God wants you to be awakened to the dangers that CBDCs represent. In Genesis 6:13-14, God warned Noah of an impending flood that would destroy all life on earth. God instructed Noah to build an ark and gather two of every kind of animal, male and female, to survive the flood.

Noah obeyed God's command and spent years constructing the massive ark. He gathered the animals, as well as his family, which included his wife, his sons Shem, Ham, Japheth and their wives. As the rains began to fall and the floodwaters rose, Noah and his family and all the animals were safe inside the ark. The flood lasted for 40 days and 40 nights, covering the entire earth. Finally, the floodwaters receded, and the ark came to rest on the mountains of Ararat. Noah then sent out a dove to see if the waters had receded enough for the birds to find dry land. The dove returned with an olive leaf, a sign that there was indeed dry land.

Noah and his family and all the animals then disembarked from the ark and began to repopulate the earth. God made a covenant with Noah, promising to never again destroy all life on earth with a flood. The story of Noah's Ark is a powerful reminder of God's love and mercy, as well as His judgement. It teaches us the importance of obedience to God and the value of righteousness in a world that can be full of wickedness. At this moment in time, God is warning us of the impending CBDC mark of the beast financial system that governments and central banks across the world have started implementing to enslave mankind.

What Is A CBDC?

A Central Bank Digital Currency (CBDC) refers to a novel type of digital money that is issued by a central bank rather than a commercial bank. In this scenario, the Bank of England (BoE) is the institution involved, as opposed to banks like Lloyds, Halifax or Barclays. A CBDC differs from traditional currency in that it is not available in physical form as notes and coins. Instead, it exists solely in digital format and can be accessed and displayed through electronic devices such as computers, phones or other similar devices. CBDC payments, being facilitated by state-owned banks, enable the government to have oversight over the financial transactions of the public.

CBDCs are unlike cryptocurrencies like Bitcoin, which are a type of digital currency that can be traded and exchanged without the need for a third-party intermediary. CBDCs are gaining significant popularity, with more than 90 central banks currently engaged in research, development or pilot programmes for their implementation. However, the hasty implementation of a new digital pound poses a threat to the privacy of the general public. The widespread adoption of any centralised digital currency will have a significant impact on the amount of data generated by everyday transactions. Consequently, it will also affect the extent to which the state can access the public's identity, income and transaction history and information. This situation poses serious risks of state surveillance.

Mark of The Beast Patent Number: WO 2020/060606 A1

As the COVID-19 (CV-19) plandemic was in full swing, Microsoft published a patent for a *"CBDC currency system using body activity data"*. This patent is filed under the number WO 2020 060606 A1 which integrates 5G, CBDC,

Nanotech and Vaccines. The number WO2020060606A1 contains three "6s" which is the obvious number of the mark of the beast "666" (Revelation 13:18).

Here is wisdom. Let him that hath understanding count the number of the beast: for it is the number of a man; and his number is Six hundred threescore and six.

Revelation 13:18

This patent focuses on tracking body activity using nano tech and nano particles (graphene oxide) via vaccines. It can also be implemented via implanted microchips. The spread of the CV-19 plandemic in 2020 sparked a flurry that exposed the planned agenda of injecting people with a deadly vaccine mixed with graphene oxide. Bill Gates, Klaus Schwab and a host of powers-that-shouldn't be had started the plandemic so that he could insert nano particles into people around the globe under the guise of providing vaccinations. In April 2020, the patent owned by Microsoft came to light that pertained to the micro-chipping of individuals for financial gain and control. This patent was especially insidious, because it carried the numbers "666", the Biblical "mark of the beast", and the letters WO, which stood for "World Order".

He that hath an ear, let him hear what the Spirit saith unto the churches; To him that overcometh will I give to eat of the tree of life, which is in the midst of the paradise of God.

Revelation 2:7

(12) INTERNATIONAL APPLICATION PUBLISHED UNDER THE PATENT COOPERATION TREATY (PCT)

(19) World Intellectual Property
Organization
International Bureau

(43) International Publication Date
26 March 2020 (26.03.2020)

WIPO | PCT

(10) International Publication Number
WO 2020/060606 A1

(51) International Patent Classification:
G06Q 20/06 (2012.01)   *G06Q 30/02* (2012.01)
G06Q 20/32 (2012.01)   *G06N 3/08* (2006.01)
H04L 9/32 (2006.01)

(21) International Application Number:
PCT/US2019/038084

(22) International Filing Date:
20 June 2019 (20.06.2019)

(25) Filing Language: English

(26) Publication Language: English

(30) Priority Data:
16/138,518   21 September 2018 (21.09.2018)   US

(71) Applicant: **MICROSOFT TECHNOLOGY LICENSING, LLC** [US/US]; One Microsoft Way, Redmond, Washington 98052-6399 (US).

(72) Inventors: **ABRAMSON, Dustin**; Microsoft Technology Licensing, LLC, One Microsoft Way, Redmond, Washington 98052-6399 (US). **FU, Derrick**; Microsoft Technology Licensing, LLC, One Microsoft Way, Redmond, Washington 98052-6399 (US). **JOHNSON, Joseph Edwin, JR.**; Microsoft Technology Licensing, LLC, One Microsoft Way, Redmond, Washington 98052-6399 (US).

(74) Agent: **MINHAS, Sandip S.** et al.; Microsoft Technology Licensing, LLC, One Microsoft Way, Redmond, Washington 98052-6399 (US).

(81) Designated States *(unless otherwise indicated, for every kind of national protection available)*: AE, AG, AL, AM, AO, AT, AU, AZ, BA, BB, BG, BH, BN, BR, BW, BY, BZ, CA, CH, CL, CN, CO, CR, CU, CZ, DE, DJ, DK, DM, DO, GB, GD, GE, GH, GM, GT, HN, HR, HU, ID, IL, IN, IR, IS, JO, JP, KE, KG, KH, KN, KP, KR, KW, KZ, LA, LC, LK, LR, LS, LU, LY, MA, MD, ME, MG, MK, MN, MW, MX, MY, MZ, NA, NG, NI, NO, NZ, OM, PA, PE, PG, PH, PL, PT, QA, RO, RS, RU, RW, SA.

(54) Title: CRYPTOCURRENCY SYSTEM USING BODY ACTIVITY DATA

---

(54) Title: CRYPTOCURRENCY SYSTEM USING BODY ACTIVITY DATA

Mark of The Beast Patent Number: WO 2020/060606 A1

Why CBDCs Are Paving Way For The Mark of The Beast System To Be Implemented

CBDCs are paving the way for the mark of the beast system to be implemented because this patent paves the way for people to be linked through a 5G technology and vaccines in order to access their money in a bank. This will be used to allow buying and selling using CBDCs.

In Revelation 13:16-18, the Bible says...

And he (antichrist) causeth all, both small and great, rich and poor, free and bond, to receive a mark in their right hand, or in their foreheads: And that no man might buy or sell, save he that had the mark, or the name of the beast, or the number of his name. Here is wisdom. Let him that hath understanding count the number of the beast: for it is the number of a man; and his number is Six hundred threescore and six.

'Implanted Under Your Skin' If You Want To Access Your Bank Accounts

On July 10th 2023, the WEF (World Economic Forum) announced that in the near future, all citizens will be required to have a CBDC microchip implanted. This will enable them to fully engage in society and carry out essential activities like buying food and water. According to Professor Richard Werner, in the near future, individuals will require the use of advanced technology, like a CBDC chip implant, to access their bank accounts.

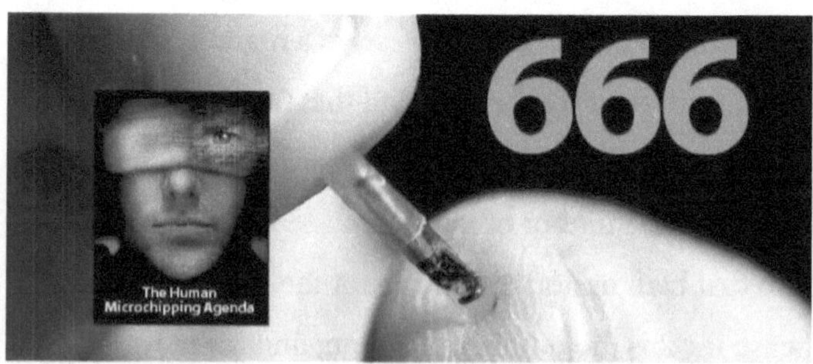

Mark of the beast microchip implant

Professor Richard A. Werner is an economist and a professor specialising in the fields of banking and finance. He gained recognition as the advocate for a monetary policy known as Quantitative Easing (QE). QE in simple terms means printing money out of thin air.

He introduced this policy in Japan in 1995 while serving as the chief economist of a British investment bank. According to a report from Expose-news.com... During the Amsterdam Science Summit 2022, Professor Werner delivered a lecture focusing on central bank digital currencies and their relationship with the United Nations (UN) 2030 Agenda. Agenda 2030 is the idea of secretly forming a totalitarian world government and a New World

Order (NWO). It is about conspiring to eventually achieve world domination and rule the world through an authoritarian one-world government—which will replace sovereign nation-states. During the Amsterdam Science Summit, he had a conversation with Ivor Cummins regarding CBDCs and the central banks' use of high inflation to advance their agenda.

Prof. Werner proposed two aspects of QE monetary policies: QE1 and QE2. Quantitative Easing 1 (QE1) involves the central bank intervening by purchasing non-performing assets within the banking system (aka printing money out of thin air). The central bank resolves the issue by purchasing non-performing assets at their full face value, resulting in banks having a robust balance sheet. However, simply doing that will not be sufficient to persuade banks to raise credit limits. Professor Werner proposed a concept called QE2, which grants the central bank the authority to compel banks to generate additional money and inject it into the economy. This can be achieved by central banks purchasing assets such as property, from non-bank sectors.

The funds obtained from the sale of the property by non-bank sectors will be subsequently transferred to the seller's bank account. According to Professor Werner, when an economy is facing deflation, central banks have the ability to inject (print more) money directly into the economy.

Japan followed QE1 in the 1980s, but the USA later disallowed Japan from using QE2. Unexpectedly and in an untimely manner, the US Federal Reserve and other central banks adopted QE2 in March 2020. The intention behind adopting QE2 at that time was to deliberately bring about high inflation. Why? To transition economies onto a Central Bank Digital Currency (CBDC) mark of the beast financial system.

According to Professor Werner, it is important to view CDBCs as a control system or permit system rather than a currency. It is a conditional currency that depends on your successful acquisition of the permit. If you happen to be a critic of government policy or central banks, you'll be denied access to your money. If you are willing to venture beyond the boundaries of the 15-minute city zone, you might discover that your CBDC will not work. Certainly, these are experiences that we have already witnessed in China. There are numerous videos available where individuals attempt to use their social credit scores to purchase tickets, only to find that it doesn't work due to their low scores.

Furthermore, it is important to note that there is essentially no genuine right to appeal. In a system where a small group of individuals have control over a large population, the controllers will utilise computers and algorithms to manage the system. If you decide to appeal the blocking of CDBCs, please be aware that you will be interacting with automated responses. Professor Werner explained that he refers to the central planners as individuals who orchestrate inflation (money printing) in order to conceal changes made to banking systems. In the 1970s, high inflation was deliberately used as a strategy to hide the transition from the gold-backed US dollar to the petrodollar.

The high inflation observed in 2021/2022 was intentionally caused in order to hide and conceal the transition from the petrodollar to central bank digital currencies. In March 2020, the Federal Reserve and other major central banks like the Bank of England implemented QE2, a measure aimed at printing more money out of thin air into the economy.

It was evident that it would lead to inflation. According to Professor Werner, this was not a mistake in judgement; rather, it was done intentionally. The policy is highly specific and frequently implemented. Professor Werner stated that there is evidence to support the claim that this action was intentional.

He pointed out that in August 2019, just prior to the onset of the CV-19 plandemic, a conference was held in Jackson Hole for the annual Central Bankers conference. Notably, BlackRock, a major asset manager, was invited to attend this conference. BlackRock presented a proposal suggesting that in the event of another crisis, it would be beneficial to intentionally create inflation. They never provide an explanation; instead, they simply state that we need to generate inflation. And here's our plan for how we're going to accomplish it. They referenced his proposal, but didn't mention his name. And there is another factor, Professor Werner stated. In March 2020, the Federal Reserve hired Blackrock to purchase assets.

Quantitative easing (QE) was initially intended to address deflationary situations. However, the implementation of QE in practise was to lead to inflation, leaving little room for doubt. They were aware of it because they explicitly mentioned it. The current inflation is intentionally created by central banks and central planners. How should we go about administering punishment for their actions? Oh, let's grant them additional powers, let's provide them with unprecedented control over various aspects, including life on Earth, by means of central bank digital currencies. I believe the main reason they desired this inflation is to conceal the gradual decline of the petrodollar and facilitate the transition to a new system that is centred around Central Bank Digital Currencies.

Currently, there is discussion surrounding the utilisation of Central Bank Digital Currencies through mobile applications. Yes, that is the initial phase. The ultimate goal and what they truly desire is to implant a tiny grain of rice-sized CBDC chip under your skin.

And he causeth all, both small and great, rich and poor,
free and bond, to receive a mark in their right hand, or in
their foreheads.

Revelation 13:16

As there is a significant challenge in persuading people to accept this idea, they are leveraging crises, disruption and unemployment as a means to introduce universal basic income, with the intention of gradually familiarising the public with the idea of accepting a CBDC chip implanted under their skin.

You will receive a monthly deposit of £2,000 into your account. However, in order to optimise efficiency, they might suggest, *"We should utilise the most advanced technology, such as the CBDC chip implant"*.

Reasons To Oppose The Government's Plans For A UK CBDC

1. A Solution In Search Of A Problem

The introduction of a UK CBDC would significantly influence the nation. There is not enough evidence to justify implementing such a substantial change that would completely alter the financial landscape, put privacy and various human rights at risk, introduce security vulnerabilities, and potentially redefine the relationship between citizens and the state in an irreversible manner. The UK CBDC proposal was described by Parliament's Economic Affairs Committee as a *"solution in search of a problem"*.

2. Programmable Money And Financial Control

Programmable money and financial control are two interconnected concepts that have gained significant attention in recent years. The ability to programme the public's personal finances or welfare payments has the potential to result in financial control, invasion of privacy and even a violation of the right to protection of property.

Depending on the limitations imposed, CBDCs pose a significant risk to various other fundamental rights, such as freedom of expression, freedom of assembly and protection from discrimination. In recent years, there has been a growing trend of private and state actors targeting money as a means to shut down and digitally de-bank campaigners, effectively silencing their voices. The Canadian Government, as an illustration, utilised emergency powers to freeze the bank accounts of individuals who opposed vaccine mandates. PayPal recently terminated the account of a journalist and advocate for free speech based in the UK.

3. Digital ID, CBDC And Discrimination

Issuing a UK CBDC without a comprehensive digital identity system is nearly impossible. The combination of digital identity and CBDCs presents significant risks such as surveillance, security breaches, hacking, identity theft and discrimination. Every individual should be entitled to access the economy, regardless of whether they possess digital currency or a digital ID. There would be an implementation of "tiered wallets" that would enable individuals with limited forms of identification to open basic digital pound wallets. These wallets would allow for limited and low-value payments.

Implementing a system that offers different levels of access to funds based on the amount of identification provided is a discriminatory practise, resembling an identity paywall. This approach would disproportionately impact marginalised groups, older individuals and those with lower incomes, as they are less likely to possess advanced forms of identification.

4. Invasion of Privacy

Given the current legal landscape, which includes counter-terror law, anti-money laundering law, and investigatory powers law, there would be widespread surveillance of CBDC transactions. Every transaction will be recorded, and anyone with access to the core ledger, whether it be a public authority or a hacker, would have the potential to view these transactions.

5. Security Risks

A centralised CBDC system would establish a significant platform for population data, making it a crucial component of national infrastructure. Having a large target like this would make it easier for hostile state and non-state actors to focus their cyberattacks. The combination of digital identity and CBDC presents a significant risk of security breaches, hacking and identity theft. If a breach were to occur, it could potentially endanger the entire public.

6. Data Exploitation

Data exploitation refers to the act of utilising data for various purposes. The act of exploiting personal data in this manner would support and encourage mass surveillance and the exploitation of sensitive personal information belonging to the public. This would result in further reduction of privacy within an expanding digital prison.

Key Takeaways

God is warning us of the coming CBDC mark of the beast financial system that governments and central banks across the world have started implementing to enslave mankind. CBDC payments, being facilitated by private-owned banks (disguised as state-owned banks), will enable the government to have oversight over your financial transactions.

Microsoft published a patent for a *"CBDC currency system using body activity data"*. This patent is filed under the number WO 2020 060606 A1 which integrates 5G, CBDC, Nanotech and Vaccines. The number WO2020060606A1 contains three "6s" which is the number of the mark of the beast "666". On July 10th 2023, the WEF (World Economic Forum) announced that in the near future, all citizens will be required to have a CBDC microchip implanted. This will enable them to fully engage in society and carry out essential activities like buying food and water.

CHAPTER 2

The Greatest Threat To Our Liberty, Privacy And Future Prosperity

The most dangerous form of political coercion is economic warfare

CBDCs are the greatest threat we face to our liberty, privacy and future prosperity. CBDCs can be used to freeze your funds anytime they want to. 30 years ago, the government dealt with "domestic threats" by using the mighty force of the militarized police to take people out.

Very soon, they won't need to send in SWAT teams to punish political dissidents. They won't even need to speak to anyone. The newest and most dangerous form of political coercion is economic warfare. We got a small glimpse of it in Canada in 2022. Hundreds of citizens who donated to the Truckers For Freedom had the funds in their bank accounts frozen without any court order or just cause. But that wasn't an isolated incident. People who speak against government's propaganda on social media will be fined £2,000 ($2,500) if they have a paypal account.

PayPal has become notorious for booting people off their network and closing their accounts for no good reason. But I think one of the scariest examples of a government censoring activists, dissidents, protesters and more is how banks in Great Britain shut down and denied the account of various people. After pressure from activist groups, banks terminated people's account, but didn't give them their money. They tried transferring the money to another bank, but were again denied. People still hasn't received their funds. Now imagine a world where you don't even have another bank to go to - you have just one bank account from one banking institution that has a monopoly on money.

And imagine that this money is completely digital and can only be programmed by the bank. This is what's coming with central bank digital currencies. They wouldn't have to pester political opponents using force - they would be able to hit you where it really hurts, your wallet, with just a few keystrokes. Can you see how it will give the central bank, the Bank of England (BoE), the power to freeze, shut down or steal your money? Isn't it obvious that they will expand this power to force as many people in society to do what they're told without resorting to direct violence? CBDCs are the greatest threat we face to our liberty, privacy and future prosperity and it is definitely preparing a way for the mark of the beast financial system...

And it was given unto him to make war with the saints, and to overcome them: and power was given him over all kindreds, and tongues, and nations. And all that dwell upon the earth shall worship him, whose names are not written in the book of life of the Lamb slain from the foundation of the world. If any man have an ear, let him hear.

Revelation 13:7-9

The End Game In Sight: The New World Order Being Ushered In Through Finance & Commerce

With CBDCs people will no longer be free. Don't be misled by promises of safety, anonymity and protection of your information. All of these things are lies and distractions meant to hide the evil intentions behind the global rollout of CBDCs.

Central Bank Digital Currency is the most complete, far-reaching and authoritarian way to keep people in line that has ever been thought of. Because of its "interoperability", CBDCs from different national central banks will be able to be linked together to form a single, centralised global system for monitoring and controlling CBDCs. If we let it win, CBDCs will give the power to run the world to the banksters and eventually the antichrist.

And the dragon was wroth with the woman, and went to make war with the remnant of her seed, which keep the commandments of God, and have the testimony of Jesus Christ.

Revelation 12:17

CBDCs are not like any other kind of "money" that we know. It can be programmed, and "smart contracts" that control the terms and conditions of a transaction can be written into its code. CBDCs can be used to enforce policy decisions and larger policy goals that can limit your life in any way that is wanted. CBDC will make it possible to keep an eye on you and manage you in ways that have never been done before. Every transaction you make will be watched and controlled. The central banksters of the global governance state will keep an eye on not only the things you buy, but also the deals you make with others. The collection of data will grow to include every part of your life.

This will make it possible for central planners (minions of the ant-christ) to shape society the way banksters and eventually the anti-christ want. CBDCs will be tied to your Digital ID, as well as to your personal carbon credit accounts and jab/vaccine certificates, and they will be. CBDCs will limit how much you can move around and give the programmers the power to change how you act if you stray. The goal of CBDC is to set up a dictatorship's harsh rules. If we let CBDC be our only way to get money, it will be used to enslave us. The end game of the mark of the beast is CBDCs.

CBDCs Are A Financial Transaction Control Grid

It feels as though we are being enclosed within a cage, with CBDCs and vaccine passports or digital IDs serving as the final barrier. Many people find it challenging to comprehend the potential risks associated with the current situation. We have become accustomed to the freedom of financial transactions and may not realise that if this freedom is taken away, we will be subject to a system where central banks control our assets and dictate how and where we can spend our money. It is crucial to comprehend that central bank digital currencies are not actual currencies. Instead, they function as a financial transaction control grid that enables central banksters to establish and enforce rules centrally.

This has been publicly acknowledged by the central banksters themselves. If you do not behave, your money may be shut off. Ultimately, the individual or group that holds power over the financial system wields significant influence over the economy and consequently the populace.

The Concept Of Weaponized CBDCs Is Being Discussed In Some Circles

CBDCs will potentially facilitate easy surveillance of citizens. The implementation of programmable central bank digital currency in any nation may pose a challenge for individuals seeking to maintain the confidentiality of their financial data.

The potential misuse of programmable CBDC as a spying tool is a concern, as it could be easily weaponized to halt politically unpopular activity.

The concept of a central bank digital currency is gaining popularity worldwide as governments strive to maintain and expand their financial authority. This programmable currency, controlled by the government, has the potential to serve as a surveillance tool due to its ease of use.

The Piece Of The CBDC Conundrum

The control grid that makes CBDCs so dangerous is made of many different puzzle pieces that need to fit together just right to make the digital prison complete. CBDCs themselves are just one piece. A digital wallet installed on smartphones or embedded in your body is another (*receiving a mark in their right hand or in their foreheads... Revelation 13:16*). A social credit score to measure your behaviour is another piece. But everybody knows about these. What most people don't realize is all of these small, individual pieces of the CBDC control grid need an environment to operate within. That environment is cities, and even some suburbs, especially those surrounding major cities. Because in a city, you're surrounded mostly by businesses forced to comply with the CBDC control grid and by people who are gladly using CBDCs every single day without thinking about them.

The CBDC system and all its various pieces come together perfectly within a city environment - the final and most important piece of the control grid puzzle. Have you heard of smart cities? These are visions of near-future cities designed with surveillance on every corner, most objects connected to the Internet of Things, and most people connected to the Internet of Bodies.

They're meant to be more connected, safer, more technologically advanced and better able to serve your needs. But in reality, they lock you into a mass surveillance technocratic nightmare. CBDCs are the missing piece to make smart cities work, and vice versa. Now recently, the newest threats are "15-minute cities", and "LTN" (low traffic neighbourhood).

I've been studying this concept for over two decades now since I first realized the comprehensive planning and climate change program in the UK, was all part of Agenda 2030. 15-minute cities are meant to keep you from straying too far from your home, providing everything you need within minutes of your house. In reality, they're meant to keep you locked down and tightly corralled for easier surveillance and control and to "protect the planet" from your car and other such nonsense. You cannot fully escape the CBDC control grid until you're literally living outside of it. Until your physical body and home are located outside of its environment.

That's why I moved from London to the countryside. Where I live, I'm safely outside of that environment and tucked away in a pocket of freedom. I want you to start thinking about doing the same. Because as I always say, the greatest tool for freedom is community. You would be wise to put yourself in a community that wants freedom rather than remaining in a place that will embrace CBDC enslavement.

Key Takeaways

CBDCs will allow banks, the government and eventually the anti-Christ to have full control over your money and can freeze or delete it, limit what you can buy or close your account for good. Track, trace and spy on everything you buy, everywhere you go and everyone you talk to and take away your right to privacy.

If you back something you believe in or break the Social Credit System, you will be punished financially. CBDCs will force you to cash out your savings account and will give hackers and data thieves access to your digital wallet. In a Chinese-style Social Credit System, the government could pay neighbours, family, and friends to watch on you and tell on you. CBDCs will lock you into an economic system that you can't get out of and that every business and person must trade in.

CHAPTER 3
BIS:
The Private Organisation
Enslaving Humanity

The ugly "Tower of Basel" is a symbol of slavery and evil!

With massive help from the BIS (Bank For International Settlements) the plandemic was shown to be what it really was, which was a huge stage show meant to draw people's attention away from the fact that criminal banksters in charge of the money system are making a deliberate push towards totalitarianism by controlling money and finances.

Who Is The BIS?

Montague Norman, who was the longest-serving governor of the Bank of England and Hjalmar Schacht, who would become Hitler's Minister of Economics, started the Bank for International Settlements in 1930.

The Bank that runs the world, but almost no one knows about it. The ugly "Tower of Basel" is a symbol of slavery and evil!

Their goal was to make it easier for Germany to pay war compensations to the winning Allies after the First World War. That was just a lie to hide what it really was and what it would be used for in the future. Norman and Schacht were both strong members of the Deep State cabal at the time, and they both knew that the BIS was going to be an important part of the final plan to take full control over supposedly sovereign countries around the world. In this way, they both agreed that there had to be a private "central" bank that kept a lot of secrets to coordinate and control the actions of all the other private central banks.

Montague Norman

Hjalmar Schacht

Montague Norman, Hjalmar Schacht & co-conspirators

Hjalmar Schacht with his boss, Adolf Hitler

If they were both still alive today, they would almost definitely be working with Klaus Schwab, Jerome Powell, Janet Yellen, Mark Carney, Bill Gates, Elon Musk and the rest of the crazy criminals who are leading the "Great Reset" and the fake climate change agenda.

The BIS is an organisation that is privately run and not accountable to the public. It is based in the city of Basel in Switzerland. The BIS controls more than 95% of the world's money supply by directly controlling 63 "member" central banks, such as the Bank of England, the Federal Reserve, South African Reserve Bank, the People's Bank of China, the Central Bank of Russian, the European Central Bank and the Reserve Bank of Australia. It also affects a lot of smaller central banks, which cover almost every country in the world.

This private organisation with a huge global reach has actually given itself diplomatic immunity to protect its obvious criminality from any kind of real investigation or public prosecution. Also, for some strange reason, the BIS doesn't have to pay any Swiss taxes at all. Lastly, and this shouldn't be a surprise to anyone, all of their regular top-level talks with governors from most central banks are completely private and held in complete secrecy. If minutes are kept at all, they are kept very carefully under wraps. Everything is done on a strict "need to know" basis, while at the same time trying to make sure that the bank comes across as a "force for good" on the world stage to the very few people who know it exists and may have found the official website. As an organisation, the BIS likes to stay under the surface and out of the way of the public's prying eyes.

Here are three excerpts from a book *"Tragedy And Hope – A History Of The World In Our Time"* written in 1966 by Professor Carroll Quigley, a fearless historian who earned the trust of the central banksters and was invited to some of their most secretive meetings. These excerpts will help you understand the real reason why the BIS exists.

Professor Carroll wrote...

1... "During the past two centuries when the peoples of the world were gradually winning their political freedom from the dynastic monarchies, the major banking families of Europe and America were actually reversing the trend by setting up new dynasties of political control through the formation of international financial combines. These banking dynasties had learned that all governments must have sources of revenue from which to borrow in times of emergency. They had also learned that by providing such funds from their own private resources, they could make both kings and democratic leaders tremendously subservient to their will".

2... "The powers of financial capitalism had another far-reaching aim, nothing less than to create a world system of financial control in private hands able to dominate the political system of each country and the economy of the world as a whole. This system was to be controlled in a feudalist fashion by the central banks of the world acting in concert, by secret agreements, arrived at in frequent private meetings and conferences. The apex of the system was the Bank for International Settlements (BIS) in Basle, Switzerland, a private bank owned and controlled by the world's central banks which were themselves private corporations. The growth of financial capitalism made possible a centralization of world economic control and use of this power for the direct benefit of financiers and the indirect injury of all other economic groups".

3... "It must not be felt that these heads of the world's chief central banks were themselves substantive powers in world finance. They were not. Rather, they were the technicians and agents of the dominant investment bankers of their own countries, who had raised them up and were perfectly capable of throwing them down. The substantive financial powers of the world were in the hands of these investment bankers (also called "international" or "merchants" bankers) who remained largely behind the scenes in their own unincorporated banks. These formed a system of international cooperation and national dominance which was more private, more powerful, and more secret than that of their agents in the central banks..."

The "investment bankers" he talks about are, of course, the crazies and psychopaths who run the Deep State today. There are people from famous business families like Rothschild, Rockefeller, Barclay, Morgan, Oppenheim, Lehman, Warburg, and Coutts among others.

But other imposing business people, like Mark Zuckerberg, Bill Gates, Jeff Bezos, Elon Musk, Larry Page, Eric Schmidt, Jamie Dimon, Larry Fink and Sergey Brin, are also part of this discriminatory stranglehold on the human race. They have been "allowed" or, in some cases, "selected" to "cash in" on this carefully planned and globalised system of corporate and financial crime.

Two Major Jobs For The BIS

There are two major jobs for the BIS to do right now. The first is to manage the money needed to bring about the totally fake Green New Deal, which is meant to stop and limit so much of the world economy over the next few years on purpose. To do this, the BIS has made a programme called the *"Green Swan"*, whose slogan is *"Central banking and financial stability in an age of climate change"*.

Aside from the fact that this is a completely thoughtless slogan (climate change has been happening naturally for thousands of years), it was made by criminal globalists to put the world into even more debt that can't be paid back while trying to de-carbonize the entire global economy, which is an unwise idea. It's all about causing global economic chaos on purpose so that the people of the world will accept the Great Reset, the Central Bank Digital Currencies and the joys of living in a corporate and digital technocracy that is carefully controlled and well-funded.

The second, and even more important, job of the Bank for International Settlement is to oversee and force the quick introduction of the Central Bank Digital Currencies (CBDC) mentioned above, while also making sure that physical cash is actively discouraged and quickly phased out. Criminal globalists have been planning for a long time for this sudden mass switch to electronic money and digital banking. This is why private high street banks are quickly closing down a large number of their local stores. It also explains why people are being forced or convinced to accept the "advantages" and "convenience" of online banking. The main reason for making this Central Bank digital currency is to be able to control every business and retail activity in the world.

This is being done by switching from a "split circuit monetary system" to one unified electronic and digital monetary system... a system that is directly controlled by the BIS. Just to remind you again, the BIS is a very secretive, private, unelected and unaccountable organisation whose criminal goal is to oversee global dictatorship. And only a tiny part of one percent of all the people in the world know anything about it! We really all need to wake up now before it is too late. Agustin Carstens, the current General Manager of the Bank for International Settlements and a close associate of the World Economic Forum said that they want to get rid of physical cash so they can rule the world and have full control over all financial transactions in the future:

"There is a huge difference between CBDC and cash. For example, with cash we don't know who's using a 100-dollar bill today. We don't know who's using a 1,000-peso bill today. A key difference with the CBDC is the central bank will have absolute control (Revelation 13:16-18) under rules and regulations that will determine the use of that expression of central bank liability (your money in the bank), and we will have the technology to enforce that".

Agustin Carstens – the current senior public figure of the criminal BIS

This rush to make big, centralised changes to how money is used and how banking works is part of a bigger plan to have total technological control over every part of our lives and how we spend our money. It is also about being able to punish! How do you get the food your family needs if those nice, controlling psychopaths decide all of a sudden that you haven't been working with them and must be punished? You will be totally cut off from the market place if you can't access any form of digital money. This can be done remotely and immediately. We've all seen how quickly your access to money can disappear when private high street banks have so-called "technical glitches". We all need to figure out this plan quickly.

A tyrannical government would be able to control every part of our lives from far away if we didn't use cash. All of us have been warned! But what will we do about it now?

Key Takeaways

The BIS is an organisation that is privately run and not accountable to the public. It is based in the city of Basel in Switzerland. The BIS controls more than 95% of the world's money supply by directly controlling 63 "member" central banks. The first major job of the BIS is to manage the money needed to bring about the totally fake Green New Deal, which is meant to stop and limit much of the world economy over the next few years on purpose.

The second job of the Bank for International Settlement is to oversee and force the quick introduction of the Central Bank Digital Currencies (CBDCs), while also making sure that physical

cash is actively discouraged and quickly
phased out.

CHAPTER 4

The Banking Contagion: Why European & US Banks Are Deliberately Been Destroyed To Usher In CBDCs

The banking crash is all planned and a deliberate attack on our liberties and freedom

Bank failures are becoming more common around the world, which is scary for people who keep their money in certain banks. The banking contagion is all planned and a deliberate attack on smaller banks, our liberty and freedom.

All of this was planned ahead of time by the global deep-state banksters. All central banks, including the Bank of England, the European Central Bank,

IMF (International Monetary Fund) and the Federal Reserve, are part of this huge group of people working together. This was already planned when they came up with the idea to leak CV-19, which they also made, and worked with the WHO (World Health Organisation) and world governments to set up lockdowns and safety measures around the world in case of a plandemic.

Don't fall for it. It was clear. It was also part of the plan to print money to destabilise global fiats and cause global inflation to rise quickly. This, along with the proxy war in Ukraine, was meant to cause food and energy shortages around the world. Then they acted like they were caught off guard and needed to raise interest rates as quickly as possible, faster than ever before in history. Which would then make the markets for business and private real estate less stable and cause the banking sector to fail. Now, they knew that this would make smaller banks fail, which would force them to be bought out or merged with bigger banks that were too big to fail. You know, the ones that former FED Chair and deep state actor Janet Yellen just happened to say she would only be bailing out of on a worldwide show.

And then she said she would let all the small banks fail. Everyone got scared and rushed to the smaller banks to get their money, but they chose to put their money in the big banks instead. All of this was also planned. They want the smaller banks to be pushed to merge with the big banks so that the big banks can get more deposits and have even more power and control over the rest of the banks. Why? Because all of these banks that are too big to fail are working together with the FED and Yellen, and they are all quietly working for the global deep-state banksters. They don't care about people at all and all they want is total control over people's financial affairs.

Because all of these big banks are on board with the next step, which is to push central bank digital currencies (CBDC). They planned to crash the whole world economy on purpose, then offer to save us with their CBDCs. The world's richest families, who run the deep state (the Illuminati), own the Bank of England, the FED and all other central banks.

And this would give them complete power and control over everyone on Earth. So, the New World Order, with its One World Government, was born. Once they get complete control over everyone through CBDCs *then the mark of the beast will be ready to be enforced.* The central banks don't really care about any one country. All of them are owned and run by some of the despicable families in the world, like the Rothschilds.

All of their love goes to these families. And they are all planning in secret to overthrow the governments of the world so that they can build the One World Government, New World Order. The London Stock Exchange, the European Stock Market and the US Securities and Exchange Commission (SEC) and market makers are also working together in secret to manipulate the stock markets and global metal markets. They give a lot of money to the deep state. If you refuse to accept their CBDC when it's rolled out, you cut off their free money and Ponzi schemes, and you're also cutting off the head of the snake. This is how you destroy the global bankster deep state from the bottom up.

If everyone around the world refuses CBDCs and works together to destroy and break up the deep states and their monopolies, we can finally bring the world's biggest families and crime syndicates to justice. And finally, bring peace to the world and make it a better place for everyone. We can all live together in a real paradise on Earth.

[1]And I saw a new heaven and a new earth: for the first heaven and the first earth were passed away; and there was no more sea. [2]And I John saw the holy city, new Jerusalem, coming down from God out of heaven, prepared as a bride adorned for her husband. [3]And I heard a great voice out of heaven saying, Behold, the tabernacle of God is with men, and he will dwell with them, and they shall be his people, and God himself shall be with them, and be their God. [4]And God shall wipe away all tears from their eyes; and there shall be no more death, neither sorrow, nor crying, neither shall there be any more pain: for the former things are passed away. [5]And he that sat upon the throne said, Behold, I make all things new. And he said unto me, Write: for these words are true and faithful.

Revelation 21:1-5

International Monetary Fund (IMF) Introduces New Global Currency to "Enslave" World Economy

Ninety-nine percent of the people in the world don't know what's going on with the new global money that just started. The "Universal Monetary Unit", also known as "Unicoin", is a "digital currency (CBDC)" issued by the International Monetary Bank (IMF). It was made to work with money from any country.

We should all be worried about this, because a lot of countries using a new "global currency" would be a big step forward for the globalist plan to implement the mark of the beast system. The IMF didn't make this new money, but it was shown off at a big IMF meeting at the International Monetary Fund (IMF) Spring Meetings 2023 that took place in Washington, D.C. on April 10-16, 2023, the Digital Currency Monetary Authority (DCMA) announced the official launch of an international central bank digital currency (CBDC) that reinforces the monetary control of participating central banks and follows the IMF's recent policy recommendations for digital currencies.

The symbol "Ü" stands for the Universal Monetary Unit (UMU), which is fiat money that can be traded for any cash settlement currency. It is a CBDC to make sure banks follow the rules and have the power on foreign banking systems to keep them under authoritarian control. This new

"Universal Monetary Unit" was made by the Digital Currency Monetary Authority.

Who Is The Digital Currency Monetary Authority (DCMA)?

The DCMA is the world's leader in supporting digital currency and new ways for governments and central banks to handle money. The DCMA is made up of sovereign states, central banks, business and private banks, and other types of financial institutions. It is a hidden group of foreign banks and national governments working together to force us to use this new currency.

The "Universal Monetary Unit" is "CDBC 2.0", and the people who made it hope that "all citizenries in a global economy" will use it. The DCMA calls the Universal Monetary Unit "CBDC 2.0" because it uses a new wave of cryptographic technologies to build a public digital currency monetary system with a framework for wide acceptance and use cases for all groups in a global economy. This is very sketchy. The Digital Currency Monetary Authority isn't the only group working on a new digital currency, of course.

One was also made in the US by the Federal Reserve Bank. The same goes for the European Union. And does it surprise anyone that the Bank of England and the UK government is talking up the possible benefits of a "digital pound" called the Britcoin?" The following is what the Bank of England website says...

"The digital pound would be a new type of money issued by the Bank of England for everyone to use for day-to-day spending. You would be able to use it in-store or online

to make payments. This type of money is known as a
central bank digital currency (CBDC). You may also hear
it being called 'digital sterling' or even 'Britcoin'. We call
the UK version of CBDC the digital pound. The digital
pound would be denominated in sterling and its value
would be stable, just like banknotes. £10 in digital pounds
would always have the same value as a £10 banknote. If
we introduced it, it would not replace cash (emphasis
added "it will definitely replace cash"). The digital pound
would be issued by the Bank of England".

Just like the UK, the Biden government
in the U.S. is also talking up the possible
benefits of a "digital form of the U.S.
dollar?" The official White House
website says the following...

"A digital money issued by the United States central bank
(CBDC) would be a digital version of the U.S. dollar.
Even though the U.S. hasn't chosen if it will go for a
CBDC yet, it has been closely looking at what it would
mean and what it could do to get one. If the U.S. went
after a CBDC, there could be many benefits, such as
making transfers faster and cheaper, making the financial

system more accessible, boosting economic growth, and making sure the U.S. stays at the centre of the international financial system (emphasis added "more control over the global financial markets"). The U.S. dollar would be turned into digital money (CBDC) by the central bank of the United States".

It's no coincidence that countries in the West are all making CBDCs at the same time. The IMF (International Monetary Fund) has already made a very thorough guide *"to help central banks and governments around the world with their CBDC rollouts"*. The IMF's plan to help CBDC rollouts is explained in the ***"IMF Approach to Central Bank Digital Currency Capacity Development"*** study, which was made public on April 10, 2023. As part of this plan, a "CBDC Handbook" is also made for monetary officials to use. People will cheer when these new digital currencies come out.

But you should know that once everyone uses them, your money will no longer be private at all. Almost everything you buy and sell will be tracked by the government, and they won't hesitate to use that against you.

The chance of tyranny is, well, off the charts in this kind of situation. Can you imagine a world where you can't buy anything for a while because you've already used up your "carbon credits" for the month? A government official could take away your "financial privileges" at any time. If you cause enough trouble, you could even be "deplatformed" from the system for good. For a system like this to really work, cash and other forms of payment will have to be taken out. This is exactly what is happening in Europe right now.

On the main page of the website for the European Parliament, it says…

"MEPs (Members of European Parliament) want to limit transactions in cash and crypto assets by putting a cap on how much money people who sell goods or services can accept. They set limits of up to €7,000 for cash payments and €1,000 for crypto-asset trades where the customer can't be named".

In the end, they'll just keep dropping the amounts until almost no one uses cash anymore. Slowly but surely, they will force everyone to use the new CBDC digital beast system, which they will control with an iron hand. Most people will be glad to help. Most people barely make it from one month to the next these days, and a recent study found that 70% of most people are "financially stressed" right now. Because of inflation, uncertain economies and not saving and investing enough, more and more people worry about their finances. 70% of most adults are worried about their own finances right now, and 52% of adults said their worries have gotten worse since before the CV-19 plandemic began in March 2020. Most people don't care that these new CBDC digital currencies could make people's lives challenging.

They just want to be able to take care of their families and pay their bills. If our leaders tell them that this new method will help the economy, they will be all for it. But those of us who are aware (of the mark of the beast system) know that more globalism doesn't lead anywhere good. Putting even more power in the hands of the foreign unelected powers-that-shouldn't be is never a good idea, and I hope that more people will start to understand this.

SWIFT Plans Launching CBDC Platform In 12-24 Months

On March 25th 2024, SWIFT, the global bank messaging network, announced plans to launch a CBDC platform within the next 12-24 months, to connect the upcoming wave of central bank digital currencies now in development to the existing financial system. It is worth noting that a significant number of central banks worldwide are currently investigating the possibility of introducing digital versions of their currencies. According to Nick Kerigan, SWIFT's head of innovation, the recent trial conducted by the company was a significant achievement. The trial lasted for 6 months and included a diverse group of central banks, commercial banks and settlement platforms. This collaboration was one of the largest in the world focused on CBDCs and "tokenised" assets.

Kerigan mentioned that the results of the project were considered successful by the participants and have provided SWIFT with a clear timeline to follow. It was noted that banks can utilise their current infrastructure for this purpose. "We are currently developing a plan to launch our product within the next 12-24 months", Kerigan stated during an interview. "It's progressing from an experimental stage to becoming a tangible reality".

The Bahamas, Nigeria, and Jamaica have already implemented CBDCs. China has the e-yuan. There is also ongoing development of a digital euro by the European Central Bank, and the Bank for International Settlements is conducting various cross-border trials. The latest trial included central banks from Germany, France, Australia, Singapore, Czech Republic, Thailand and several others who preferred to remain anonymous.

Several commercial banks, such as HSBC, Citibank, Deutsche Bank, Societe Generale, Standard Chartered and the CLS FX settlement platform, participated in the event. Additionally, there were also contributions from at least two banks from China.

SWIFT Steps Towards The Mark of The Beast

SWIFT's plan to launch a Central Bank Digital Currency (CBDC) platform could potentially be seen as a step towards the creation of a global, centralized mark of the beast financial system. Here are some reasons why this is a concern...

Centralization Of Power

This centralization of currency issuance and control could lead to increased power and control over the economy, financial transactions, and citizens by the central government. As more governments adopt CBDCs and these currencies become interconnected, there is a potential for a single, global centralized mark of the beast financial system.

Surveillance And Control

Digital currencies can be more easily monitored and tracked by the issuing authority, which could lead to a reduction in privacy and an increased potential for surveillance and control over you and businesses. This will align with the "Mark of the Beast", which restricts people's freedom and forces them to submit to a satanic authority.

Potential For Mandatory Participation

CBDCs could eventually become the only legal tender, forcing you to participate in the system in order to engage in commerce. This will create pressure for you to receive a unique identifier or "mark" to be able to use the currency, reminiscent of the "Mark of the Beast" concept.

Dependency On Technology

A CBDC platform relies on sophisticated technology to operate, which could be vulnerable to hacking, cyberattacks or system failures. The potential consolidation of power and control in a centralized digital currency system is seen as a step towards the creation of a global "Mark of the Beast" system.

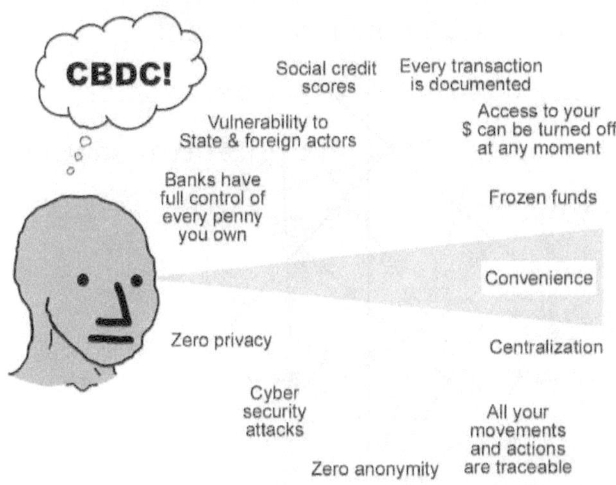

How NatWest And Major UK Banks Are Imposing Cash Limits Ready For A Cashless Society

NatWest imposes new cash limits in latest de-banking row warning that customers are being forced towards a cashless society as bank grants itself 'sweeping new powers'. They recently

acquired expanded authority to impose
restrictions on cash deposits and
withdrawals. This development is
pushing customers towards a society
that heavily relies on digital transactions
and towards a "cashless society".

NatWest has announced new limits on cash deposits and withdrawals

The bank informed its current account
holders that it will be implementing new
conditions that grant them the authority
to establish limits on both inbound and
outbound payments. They also said to be

implementing "daily and annual" limits on cash withdrawals and deposits, as well as restricting the amount of cash that can be paid in or taken out. The decision of imposing more restrictions on the use of paper currency throughout the system have adverse effects on consumers.

The revelation of Coutts, owned by NatWest Group, closing Nigel Farage's (Former UKIP Leader) account due to a disagreement over his political views has contributed to a larger scandal surrounding the practise of "de-banking". Mr Farage expressed his concern about banks granting themselves extensive powers to restrict their customers' cash usage, describing it as deeply worrying.

"The broader de-banking scandal that I have uncovered has already shown that banks cannot be relied upon to responsibly exercise such power. They have been closing people's accounts solely based on their political beliefs", he stated in an interview with The Telegraph.

Customers who violate the bank's policies may have their access to cash restricted, leading to fears among the public.

Tomorrow Begins Today

NatWest announced the changes to their terms and conditions through a leaflet titled ***"Tomorrow Begins Today"***, which was initially distributed in June, 2023. The leaflet served as a notification to customers regarding the modifications.

The rules, effective September 11, 2023 outlined that limitations may be imposed on payments made to and from your account. These limitations may include restrictions on the amount of cash you deposit or withdraw, as well as certain payment methods.

Anne-Marie Morris, a Member of Parliament from the Conservative Party who serves on the treasury committee in the House of Commons, expressed her concern by stating, *"It is important that we do not transition to a cashless society without seeking input and consent from consumers"*. Members of Parliament (MPs) have expressed concerns regarding the impact of bank branch closures and the increasing coercion for card payments imposed on businesses. These developments are leaving cash users at a disadvantage. Cash is primarily utilised by individuals who respect their privacy.

A Cashless Society Is A Dream Of The Anti-Christ

Once the anti-Christ is revealed he will be so happy that the society you and I have enjoyed so much has gone cashless because it will be easier for him to entrap people with their finances. Cashless systems let governments pick on groups they don't like by watching, managing or just stopping their spending.

Any move away from cash makes it more likely that people won't be able to get back on their feet as quickly after a disaster. Cash doesn't care who you are. It is also efficient because it circulates within economies that have been hit by disasters and has a "multiplier effect" that cashless choices that spread outside of a single economy don't have. A strong move towards a cashless society is already happening in places like China and Sweden. Cash is the only payment method that is truly safe and open to everyone. The places where financial institutions keep their data, called "data centres", can go down. No electronic payment method can be as safe as cash.

Without cash, you lose the freedom that cash gives you. Negative interest rates, which would force savers to pay banks to keep their money, are an interesting example of how cash gives people more power. With cash, you can take money out of your account and put it somewhere else, like a safety deposit box. People should be able to choose how they want to pay for their services. It's important that cash stays an option because it's the only one that gives people full control over how they pay. Cash works without the issuer and gives people control over their own money in a way that no other choice can. With a cashless society, governments will use cashless payment platforms to keep an eye on their people and give them a "social score". Too many people don't know that we're moving towards a society without cash which is a dream come true for the anti-Christ.

Why Universal Basic Income Is A Trap

The mayor of Greater Manchester, Andy Burnham, expressed that a universal basic income would provide individuals with a secure foundation, alleviating concerns and allowing them to live their lives without any worries. This statement echoes what a tyrannical government (or anti-Christ) will be fully supporting. Why? Because when you accept universal basic income you are now dependent on the state which will demand you do things that goes against your core value and your beliefs like taking the CV-19 jab.

UBI is where everyone will be given a basic income of £1,600 per month. Every month individuals will receive a lump sum of money with no conditions or obligations attached. Once society accept UBI it will be very challenging for people to give up free money. This is to prepare the groundwork for a tyrannical

government to take over and all these
ties in CBDCs mark of the beast financial
system. This has all been planned and
was part of the CV-19 plandemic. In
2020, a group of over 170 MPs and peers
made a request to the government. They
urged the government to establish a
universal basic income in response to
the CV-19 plandemic. You have to ask
yourself why 2020 and why not a year or
two early? Implementing a basic income
system in Great Britain has the potential
to trap people who will become
dependent on the system.

Scenario: How The CBDC Mark of The Beast System Will Look Like

Here's an example of how those who aren't prepared to exit the CBDC financial beast system will look like...

...When CBDCs roll out, you will get your allotted amount deposited into your digital wallet. Maybe it's from your pension. Or from your salary from your job. Or from benefit payments or from Universal Basic Income. It will roughly work the same way. You won't be allowed to save your money for very long.

It will be programmed to expire, so you'll be coerced into spending it on things you need and plenty of things you don't need or want. Also, you'll not be allowed to buy too much food or water. There has to be enough for everyone, after all. Your account is closely monitored and knows exactly what, when, and where you bought items and will restrict future purchases until at a designated future time you're allowed to buy those things again, even if you need them or want to stock up for emergencies.

Prepping is highly discouraged in a "controlled" CBDC society. And certain items are completely not allowed to be purchased at all unless you have a very high social credit score and can demonstrate enough "need" for them. Oh, and if you want to continue receiving your monthly allotment of CBDCs, you're going to have to "do your part" in protecting public health. There's a new strain of the virus circulating, so you'll need to get your 19th booster before you can get your money. It's for your own good. Plus, since you bought foodstuffs from a shop with a low social credit score, your own score is going to have to take a hit. You should shop at better stores, even if you have to pay higher prices.

With a lower social credit score, your rent/mortgage will have to be raised as well. You're not the most trustworthy tenant anymore, even if you have a history of paying on time. Then, one day, you are seen on a facial recognition camera in a public park holding a sign expressing undesirable opinions about the government. That's a major violation of public safety and civility. Your account is frozen and a significant portion of your funds are immediately withdrawn as an instant fee. No court date. No retribution. Swift "justice". And you are left feeling helpless because you have no idea what to do to escape this nightmare. Many of the things I just described are actually happening in China where a social credit score and CBDC have been merged. This system is on its way. What's happening in China, Nigeria, Jamaica and elsewhere is coming to Great Britain and a town near you!

Key Takeaways

The banking crash is all planned and a deliberate attack on smaller banks, our liberty and freedom. Natwest is pushing customers towards a society that heavily relies on digital transactions and towards a "cashless society".

If everyone around the world refuses CBDCs and works together to destroy and break up the deep states and their monopolies, we can finally bring the world's biggest families and crime syndicates to justice. Cashless systems let governments pick on groups they don't like by watching, managing or just stopping their spending. Cash is the only payment method that is truly safe and open to everyone. Without cash, you lose the freedom that cash gives you.

Something To Think About!

Many individuals, especially the elderly who do not have access to the internet, rely heavily on cash. The increasing digitalisation of everything and the move towards a cashless society may result in some individuals being excluded from fully participating in society. A cashless society implies the absence of physical currency. Cashless means fully digital, full traceable, fully controlled.

A Cashless Society Means...

- No more cash donations to a favourable cause.
- No more garage sales.
- No more cash slipped into the hands of a child from their grandparent.
- No more money in birthday cards.
- No more piggy banks or tooth fairy for your child.

- No longer selling items from your home that you no longer want/need for cash.
- Less choices of where you purchase based on affordability.

A cashless society ensures that every transaction you make is meticulously recorded, leaving behind a traceable trail of all your movements and actions. Banks have complete control over all of your funds.

CHAPTER 5

Why Cryptocurrencies Are A Threat To The Current Financial System And The Way Money Is Handled

Cryptocurrencies make it possible for people to take full control of their money for the first time in history

The Internet may be the piece of technology that has done the most to make people free. No one is in charge of the Internet. We can send and receive information around the world without asking anyone's permission, being censored or having a central authority.

Even so, the Internet may not be as open as it was meant to be right now. The Internet is less of a decentralised network now that domain names have been centralised and social media have been taken over by a few big companies. But it has still given us a lot of freedom. As George Washington said in 1788, **"Liberty is a plant that grows quickly once it has taken root".** The Internet, which is a plant that gives people freedom, has grown quickly and changed many industries. But finance has been left alone for the most part.

Cryptocurrencies such as Bitcoin, which is built on top of the Internet and can be used by anyone without permission, is probably the biggest threat to the financial system right now. And here's why. In a strange way, commercial banks make the best case for Bitcoin. Because the financial system is irrational on the inside, any slight sane alternative is a threat. Fractional reserve banking is the name for this irrational idea. Fractional reserve banking is a banking system in which banks create money out-of-thin-air and keep only a fraction of their deposits in reserve. Fractional reserve banking creates a risk of bank runs, where depositors rush to withdraw their money if they lose confidence in the bank's ability to repay them.

Satoshi Nakamoto (the creator of Bitcoin) pointed out that ***"banks must be trusted to hold and electronically transfer our money, but they lend it out in waves of credit bubbles with hardly anything in reserve"***. These credit bubbles are basically a way to make fake money. When you borrow money from a bank, the money appears out of thin air in the form of digital credit. These banks are spending money from their reputation, which is only partly backed by the money that their customers have put in. So, even though bank customers have a legal right to their property, it would be impossible to meet all of these claims at once. In fact, there have been times when all the customers asked for their money at the same time. The Greek financial crisis is a good example.

When these people asked for their money back, the bank couldn't because the customers never really had it. 35% of the ATMs ran out of money, and in the end, banks were closed for a week. The system fell apart because it was based on trust. Cryptocurrencies are the answer to this risk of fraud and gives the banking system a way to work around it. It replaces human trust with mathematical proof, making it possible for people to take full control of their digital money for the first time in history. Digital self-custody is made possible by mathematical proof of ownership, which comes in the form of digital signatures. Today, the only other way to fully control your own money is to hold cash. But this makes it impossible to make payments from afar, and it also makes the cash less secure, since it could be taken if someone broke into your house.

With Cryptocurrencies, you don't have to choose between self-storage and making payments all over the world. You get both. Cryptocurrencies are definitely a threat to the current financial system, which doesn't let people keep their own digital money and encourages digital counterfeiting. The modern financial system breaks the Cryptocurrency commandment, ***"Thou shalt not counterfeit"***. Commercial banks are the ones who do the most wrong, but they are not the only ones. Central Banks also increase the amount of money in circulation through programmes called ***"quantitative easing"***. You may have noticed that money is created out of thin air and pumped into the economy in a way that hurts everyone's savings.

In the Western world, this may not have immediate effects at first, but Venezuela shows how this works. The central bank has greatly increased the amount of money in circulation, which led to consumer prices in Venezuela growing at an astounding rate of more than 65,000% from 2017 to 2018.

It has now settled down to a mere 2,360% annually. This shows how quickly your savings can lose their worth. Hyperinflation is the rapid, massive and unmanageable increase in prices. In Hungary just after World War II, prices doubled every 15 hours. More recently, in Zimbabwe, prices doubled every day. In the troubled Yugoslavia of the 1990s, inflation hit 50% a year.

Since 1970, the U.S. dollar has lost more than 97% of its value. Between 1956 and 2022, the UK's inflation rate has been around 2,312.54%, which means the cost of living has gone up by a total of £2,312.54. In other words, £100 in 1956 was worth the same as £2,312.54 today. Between these times, the average rate of inflation per year has been 4.89 percent.

UK inflation - Conversion table

Initial Value		Equivalent value
£1 pound in 1956	→	£23.13 pounds in 2022
£5 pounds in 1956	→	£115.63 pounds in 2022
£10 pounds in 1956	→	£231.25 pounds in 2022
£50 pounds in 1956	→	£1,156.27 pounds in 2022
£100 pounds in 1956	→	£2,312.54 pounds in 2022
£500 pounds in 1956	→	£11,562.71 pounds in 2022
£1,000 pounds in 1956	→	£23,125.43 pounds in 2022
£5,000 pounds in 1956	→	£115,627.15 pounds in 2022
£10,000 pounds in 1956	→	£231,254.3 pounds in 2022
£50,000 pounds in 1956	→	£1,156,271.48 pounds in 2022
£100,000 pounds in 1956	→	£2,312,542.96 pounds in 2022
£500,000 pounds in 1956	→	£11,562,714.82 pounds in 2022
£1,000,000 pounds in 1956	→	£23,125,429.64 pounds in 2022

Source: https://www.inflationtool.com/british-pound/1956-to-present-value?amount=100&year2=2023&frequency=yearly

Since there is an unlimited amount of fiat money, it is challenging and sometimes even impossible to save for the future. On the other hand, there are only 21 million Bitcoins, which can't be made more, only given out. In the Bitcoin system, it is impossible to make fake money because everything can be checked by anyone. Since there is a public record of every transaction ever made, it is impossible to make fake money. As such, it is a way to save money that is made to keep its buying power. Bitcoin takes away the need to trust the central bank not to devalue the currency, which has happened many times in the past.

Bitcoin lets us send digitally and save without anyone's permission. Bitcoin is a threat to the central bank's ability to control all of the money. Bitcoin is not run by anyone, and it can't be inflated. The second rule of money is ***"Thou shalt not steal"***. Bitcoin is money that you can't lose without your permission. Unlike the current financial system, which is protected by flesh and blood, money that is protected by maths is completely safe. If you "own" your money in the bank, you trust the bank to give it back to you when you ask. But owning Bitcoin is what the word means in its truest form. It needs 12 or 24 words that only you know. These are your "private keys". The only way to take control of your Bitcoin is to have your private keys.

Anyone could try to guess the keys, but they would have to try one Centillion times (1 x 10^{303}). We have seen money being taken away and kept secret in the traditional financial system. Peoples money have been taken and their bank accounts frozen by governments around the world. In response, people are sending money to those affected using Bitcoin. Money that can't be taken away is messing up a system where taking money away is possible and sometimes very common. No amount of violence will ever solve a maths problem with cryptography.

The Joseph's Plan

In Genesis 41:33-57, after Joseph interpreted Pharaoh's dreams, he advised him to appoint a wise and discerning man to oversee the land of Egypt and to collect one-fifth (20%) of the harvest during the seven years of abundance. This food would then be stored up to provide for the people during the seven years of famine that would follow.

Pharaoh was pleased with Joseph's plan and appointed him to be the one in charge. Joseph was thirty years old at the time. Over the next seven years,

Joseph oversaw the collection and storage of food. He also appointed commissioners over the land to help him carry out Pharaoh's plan. When the seven years of famine came, the people of Egypt were hungry. They cried out to Pharaoh for food.

Pharaoh told them to go to Joseph and do whatever he told them. Joseph opened the storehouses and sold grain to the Egyptians. People from all over the world came to Egypt to buy grain from Joseph, because the famine was severe everywhere. Joseph's plan saved the people of Egypt from starvation. He also helped to establish Egypt as a powerful and wealthy nation.

Lessons From The Joseph's Plan

- God can use even the most challenging circumstances to accomplish His purposes.
- It is important to be wise and be prepared for the future.
- We should always be willing to help those in need.

How Joseph's Plan Applies To Us Today

The story of Joseph's plan is a reminder that God is always in control, even when things seem challenging. He can use any situation to work out his good purposes for our lives. The story also teaches us the importance of being wise and be prepared for the future. You should not wait until a crisis like the anti-Christ's mark of the beast financial system strikes to start planning. You should store up a financial resource (cryptocurrency) that will provide you with an escape route to prosper during the days you will not be able to buy and sell during the antichrist's reign.

We should also be willing to help those in need, even if it means sacrificing our own comfort or resources. Just as Joseph helped to save the people of Egypt from starvation, we can also make a difference in the world by helping others in need. We can do this by volunteering our time to educate as many people about the importance of cryptocurrencies to set us free from the financial beast system.

Top 5 Ways Cryptocurrencies Changes The World For The Better

1. Cryptocurrencies Promotes Financial Sovereignty And Is Good For Financial Independence

More than half of the world's people live in countries that have some kind of financial repression, like capital controls. Even in countries that are said to be economically free, ordinary people have to deal with the risk of bank failures or government restrictions on their money. Cryptocurrencies gives people power over their assets and makes them independent of banks and other financial institutions. This gives people the power to handle their own money without the help of a third party.

Cryptocurrencies are "unstoppable" form of money that protects both people and society from all kinds of financial repression. This makes it the basis of peace and prosperity itself.

2. Cryptocurrencies Promotes Economic Stability

Gold has been the best way to save money for most of human history. Gold gave people the freedom to focus on providing value in their trade or business instead of thinking about what to do with their savings. It did this by making sure that money saved today would have the same or more buying power in the future.

In the digital age, it's challenging to do business with gold, which makes it less useful as a source of value. Because you can't really buy anything with gold today, it's also not used as a source of value by many people. Most people instead use "fiat" currencies like the Pound, Dollar, the Euro and the Yen. We get paid with these government-issued debt bills, and we have to use them to trade with each other.

The concern is that (on purpose) the value of these currencies is always going down. High inflation is now a world-wide challenge. The average inflation rate around the world, they claim is 7.4%, and now more than a billion people live in places where inflation is in the double digits. Because the value of the money we earn keeps going down, we have no choice but to risk our hard earned money on the financial markets.

Even so, most of us are too busy with our day jobs to become experts. This leads to illogical investments and wild speculative bubbles. Cryptocurrencies bring back the idea of money as a long-term source of value because it is better than gold in several key ways. If it is able to do this, the economy will grow more slowly and steadily, and there will be fewer speculation bubbles.

3. Cryptocurrencies Reduces Corruption

Good cryptocurrency networks are not owned or run by anyone, and there is no CEO. Instead, the network is made up of people who want to be there and join on their own. Changes to the network must be agreed upon by all of its users, and there are many different opinions that can be heard. This is very different from government money, which is usually released by fiat and controlled by a small group of banksters. And in a currency system, the people who are closest to the people who print the money often do the best. Cryptocurrencies can't help insiders because it's a decentralised currency with a decentralised way of running things. Also, because certain cryptocurrency transfers can be seen by anyone, it would be very challenging to use the network to help with corruption.

4. Cryptocurrencies Promotes Financial Inclusion

In 2021, 24% of people around the world still did not have a bank account. Even though bank accounts are still extremely challenging to get in many places,

Cryptocurrencies let anyone with a mobile device that can connect to the internet join the global economy. This is a big deal for people who don't have banks or don't have enough money in them. Cryptocurrencies helps marginalised communities grow their economies and get out of poverty, whether it's a freelancer getting paid by clients around the world or a foreign worker sending money home (with lower fees than with traditional remittance services).

5. Cryptocurrencies Promotes Free Speech

The Human Rights Foundation says that 54% of the world's people live in what they call "authoritarian regimes". Freedom of speech restrictions are one

of the most autocratic things about
authoritarian regimes, which use them
to shut down dissent. When people get
together to fight against
authoritarianism, they need money.
Because of this, money is often used as
an easy way for regimes to tighten their
grip. People who are against the
government usually have their bank
accounts frozen and their assets taken
away. There are many examples of
people using cryptocurrencies to fight
back against tyranny. Money that can't
be censored can be an important way to
fight against authoritarianism.

	Bitcoin	Fiat	Gold	Real estate
Scarce	✓✓✓	✓	✓✓	✓✓
Easily divisible	✓✓✓	✓✓✓	✓✓	✗
Durable	✓✓✓	✓✓✓	✓✓✓	✓
Easy to transact	✓✓	✓✓✓	✓	✗
Portable domestically	✓✓✓	✓✓✓	✓✓	✗
Portable internationally	✓✓✓	✓	✓	✗
Easy to verify authenticity	✓✓✓	✓	✗	✓✓
Can trade large amounts without affecting price	✓✓	✓✓✓	✓✓✓	✓✓✓
Price is not volatile	✗	✓✓✓	✓✓	✓
Resistance to seizure or confiscation	✓✓✓	✓	✓	✗
Low barrier to entry (anyone can buy and small amounts are ok)	✓✓	✓✓✓	✓	✗
Increases in value over time	✓✓✓	✗	✓	✓✓✓
TOTAL SCORE:	30	25	19	12

Bitcoin, Fiat, Gold and Real Estate Comparison

Key Takeaways

Cryptocurrencies are the answer to the risk of fraud and gives the banking system a way to work around it. It replaces human trust with mathematical proof, making it possible for people to take full control of their digital money for the first time in history. Digital self-custody is made possible by mathematical proof of ownership, which comes in the form of digital signatures.

Cryptocurrencies are a threat to the current financial system, which doesn't let people keep their own digital money and encourages digital counterfeiting. The modern financial system breaks the Cryptocurrency commandment, ***"Thou shalt not counterfeit"***. With Bitcoin it is impossible to make fake money because everything can be checked by anyone.

Bitcoin takes away the need to trust the central bank not to devalue the currency, which has happened many times in the past. Bitcoin let us send digitally and save without anyone's permission. Bitcoin is a threat to the central bank's ability to control all of the money. Bitcoin is not run by anyone, and it can't be inflated.

CHAPTER 6

A New Kind Of Freedom: Why Private Cryptocurrencies Is Our Rebellion

Private cryptocurrencies are a new idea that could help you create a private, prosperous, and free life outside of the mark of the beast system

During the financial crisis of 2007/2008, Satoshi Nakamoto came up with a new way to keep monetary transfers safe by using a democratic, decentralised network. This crisis was caused by banks' risky loan practises and their willingness to take risks. Even though these banks did these things, the government still bailed them out. Because of this, people around the world

lost trust in the banking system and took
to the streets to protest.

*Protestors on the street during the 2007/2008 financial crisis
caused by the greedy banksters.*

Cryptocurrencies gives people an
alternative to the challenges with the
banking system. Cryptocurrencies has
shown that it is possible for the financial
industry to be less centralised. Also, it
shows that a money system that gives
people more power is possible.
Cryptocurrencies are designed to take
power away from a few groups and give

it to a lot of people. Because of this,
Cryptocurrencies has grown to be used
by a lot of people in a short amount of
time. Cryptocurrencies encourages
freedom and gives everyone a chance.
This digital money is similar to the
personal computer and the printing
press. So, it is a big deal.
Cryptocurrencies are a new idea that
could change how people think about
and use money. Cryptocurrencies are the
future of money because more and more
people are using it.

Private Cryptocurrencies

One of the main goals of Bitcoin (BTC)
was to be an option to government-
backed fiat money. Early on, people who
cared about privacy came to the token.
However, many later found that it didn't

protect user and transaction privacy well enough. This is partly because the token was made with a few core ideas in mind. Bitcoin and other pseudonymous cryptocurrencies are transparent because they use public blockchains. Anyone can see public addresses and activities on the network.

Standard security protocols are used to protect the wallets of these cryptocurrencies, but there are no protocols to protect the name of each user taking part in a transaction. Because of this, it is often possible to figure out who took part in a transaction by looking at its history and comparing payments and withdrawals. One thing that shows how easy it is to keep track of deals is "Whale Alert", which is a

Twitter bot that tells people when there are big changes in a number of tokens.

Reasons Why Private Cryptocurrencies Are Even More Important Than Ever In The End Times

There are several compelling reasons why privacy holds significant importance when it comes to cryptocurrency transactions. Many people fail to grasp the significance of privacy in cryptocurrency transactions. It is crucial not only for security purposes but also to safeguard personal privacy, similar to the level of privacy one experiences with traditional fiat currency transactions. Let's explore the importance of privacy in the cryptocurrency space, particularly in

light of potential threats during the end
times.

1. Financial Confidentiality

Maintaining financial confidentiality is
crucial in cryptocurrency transactions,
just as it is in traditional financial
systems. Privacy plays a vital role in
ensuring this. You have the fundamental
right to maintain the confidentiality of
your financial matters, safeguarding
both your personal and business
transactions from unwanted scrutiny.

Without privacy measures, every
transaction made on a public blockchain
would be visible to anyone. This lack of
privacy can result in unwanted exposure
and potentially harmful consequences.
For instance, criminal elements may

specifically target users who have large public balances. If certain companies have the ability to trace transactions on public blockchains and link them to you, it is also possible for other entities, including those with malicious intentions or the anti-Christ, to do the same.

2. Personal Identity Protection

Ensuring personal identity protection is crucial when it comes to everyday financial transactions. In the current era of digital technology, where a significant portion of our financial transactions take place online, it is of utmost importance to prioritise the protection of personal information in order to prevent unauthorised access. Ensuring privacy in cryptocurrency transactions is crucial for safeguarding personal identities. The transparency of transactions could potentially link your financial activities to your real-world identity, which could pose privacy risks. Cryptocurrencies are designed to offer pseudonymity, enabling you to carry out transactions without revealing your personal information unless you choose to disclose it voluntarily. Cryptocurrency projects that prioritise the privacy of their community by implementing strong security measures and encryption protocols are able to build a reputation for themselves. This reputation helps them attract and retain a loyal following.

3. Financial Inclusion

Ensuring privacy in cryptocurrency transactions is crucial for fostering financial inclusion. A significant number of people around the world lack access to conventional banking services and therefore turn to cryptocurrencies as an alternative. By preserving their privacy, individuals can engage in the digital economy while minimising unnecessary risks to their personal information.

Privacy in cryptocurrency transactions is not just a choice, but a crucial aspect for ensuring security, financial confidentiality and personal privacy. It is comparable to the level of privacy that you have when conducting transactions with traditional fiat currency. By implementing robust privacy measures, you can be protected from potential threats of being cancelled from the financial system. Additionally, your personal information and financial activities are safeguarded, which contributes to creating a safer and more inclusive digital financial ecosystem during the end times.

4. The Incoming Wave Of CBDCs

The fact that blockchain is transparent and can't be changed gives a central bank a way to track citizens' activities, making financial privacy nearly impossible. With China, which isn't known for being accepting or caring much about people's right to privacy, there are questions about how CBDCs could be used in an immoral way to keep people in line as I've already explained in previous chapters. In fact, a CBDC fits right into the social scoring system that lowers a person's score if they do not act well around other people. And in the end, it's up to the government to decide what's good social behaviour. It's not surprising that human rights groups are always criticising the regime.

Anonymity Is King: The Top Private Cryptocurrencies

At the time of writing, four of the top private cryptocurrencies are Monero (XMR), Pirate Chain (ARRR), Zcash (ZEC) and Dero (DERO). You can learn more about Monero in my other book *"The Great Revelation"* where I talk extensively why Monero is a leading cryptocurrency focused on private and censorship-resistant transactions.

Pirate Chain (ARRR) - The Most Anonymous Crypto

Pirate Chain is designed with the goal to protect financial privacy just like Monero. Pirate Chain is the first cryptocurrency to use the strongest and most well-known privacy algorithm in the industry, zk-SNARK (Zero Knowledge-Succinct Non-interactive Argument of Knowledge), in a way that can only be used privately. By default, no one can see your wallet address or any of your activities. This information is only known to the people involved in the transaction, who can choose not to keep it private by showing the transaction ID as proof of the transaction.

Pirate Chain turns the privacy business on its head and gives you back power over your privacy by giving you an option to opt out. After a public statement, Pirate Chain was pretty much ready to go. There were no private sales or pre-mined coins. Volunteers from all over the world work together to run Pirate Chain. Pirate Chain isn't like most other cryptocurrency projects in that it doesn't tax the mining rewards to pay for the project. All of the money has been raised through the generosity of the community.

How Pirate Chain Protect Privacy

Pirate Chain protects privacy and security in several ways...

Shielding: This security feature is like *"incognito mode"* for a transaction. Tokens are moved to a hidden network with a secret address. Shielded tokens can move easily through the network, but to interact with anything else, they must *"deshield"* and show themselves to a public blockchain.

Sapling: This blockchain protocol was made to make the zk-SNARKs (zero-knowledge succinct non-interactive argument of knowledge) method more safe, private and efficient. Sapling makes it possible to check transaction data without sharing private information like user names, transaction amounts or account balances.

Private Send Only: Most of its competitors let you choose how private your transactions are, but Pirate Chain wants to make sure that everyone stays anonymous by making private transactions the default. By giving out their transaction IDs, both the sender and the receiver can "opt out" of privacy. This keeps information from getting out by accident, keeps unscrupulous people from monitoring transactions that aren't encrypted, and gives you control over your own privacy.

Anonymity At Every Level: All Pirate Chain wallet addresses also use a privacy scheme that hides the funds from everyone except the wallet owner.

To learn more about Pirate Chain, go to **www.pirate.black**

How To Buy Pirate Chain ARRR

https://piratechain.com/blog/how-to-buy-pirate-chain-arrr

Zcash (ZEC): Cash For The New Age

Zcash is a simple and highly secure digital currency that prioritises safeguarding your privacy. You can use it for everyday purchases, sending money to friends, and even your favourite crypto applications. You can choose to store it, spend it, or send it. Zcash is a digital currency that serves as both a store of value and a means to keep your financial information private and under your control.

Zcash has been designed with the purpose of promoting and enabling economic freedom. Zcash shares similarities with Bitcoin in its design. In fact, Zcash was developed using the original Bitcoin code base. However, it distinguishes itself by incorporating a privacy technology that encrypts transaction information. This feature empowers you to protect and safeguard your assets. Zcash was developed by a team of scientists from prestigious academic and scientific institutions such as MIT and Johns Hopkins.

How Does Zcash Differ From Bitcoin?

Zcash is similar to Bitcoin, but it prioritises safeguarding your privacy rather than revealing your financial history. Bitcoin, which was introduced in 2009, marked a significant milestone as the world's first decentralised cryptocurrency. Bitcoin transactions are verified and recorded on a public blockchain, making your balances and transaction data visible to anyone worldwide. The absence of privacy served as a motivation for a team of scientists to develop a superior solution. In 2016, cryptography experts enhanced Bitcoin's open-source code by incorporating zero-knowledge proofs and other advancements, resulting in the creation of Zcash. Zcash provides users with all the conveniences of Bitcoin, while ensuring their financial information is fully encrypted for protection.

Zcash has several other significant differences worth mentioning. These include a self-funding mechanism, shorter confirmation times, the presence of a memo field and more.

Is Zcash Traceable?

Zcash transactions that are shielded provide encryption for users' addresses, transaction amounts and memo fields, ensuring complete privacy. When you utilise a shielded Zcash address for sending and receiving ZEC, your transaction history and wallet balance become untraceable. Spending cash at a store is similar to this type of transaction.

In this case, there is no publicly accessible record that reveals the origin of the money or the identity of the person who spent it. If you utilise a transparent Zcash address, your holdings and financial history become publicly accessible, similar to Bitcoin. Certain Zcash wallets have implemented a feature that automatically shields the funds they receive from transparent addresses.

Where To Use Or Spend Zcash

Zcash has been specifically designed to cater to the needs and demands of the digital era. It offers privacy, speed, flexibility and accessibility for all users. You can use it to purchase a wide range of items, ranging from bagels to vacations. You can use your mobile phone to privately pay a friend in Zcash, send money overseas, buy foodstuff or send a donation to a worthy cause.

You can utilise third-party applications such as Flexa SPEDN **(https://spedn.io)** to make payments using Zcash at various establishments. Moon is a service that enables you to use Zcash online at any location where Visa is accepted.

Pay With Zcash→**www.paywithz.cash**

Flexa SPEDN →**www.spedn.io**

Pay With Moon

→**www.paywithmoon.com**

To learn more about Zcash go to...

www.z.cash

Dero (DERO)

Dero is another type of cryptocurrency made to be safe and private. It has features like the ability to avoid blockchain analysis and make transactions that can't be tracked. Dero was released by a team of three full-time developers in December 2017. Its team have more than a decade of experience in security and many more years of experience in building blockchains.

Given how challenging the project was and how far the team got, Dero was made by people with a lot of hands-on experience in cryptography. For example, the team designed a whole new consensus mechanism in Golang, a programming language with a high level of security. Dero focuses on privacy and security and it is one of a kind because it uses Proof of Work and Proof of Stake methods, which make it safer and less likely to be attacked. It also has a built-in message system that lets you talk to other people safely. One of the most important things of Dero is that it uses CryptoNote, which is a system that hides the sender and receiver of a transaction to make sure that transactions cannot be tracked or linked.

This keeps the identities of everyone involved private and protects their privacy. It is also the first blockchain to have a peer-to-peer layer with full SSL (Secure Sockets Layer). This scrambles all of its network traffic and hides it from ISPs who want to look at the traffic. Bulletproofs are also a part of Dero and they help keep transaction fees low. Bulletproofs is an encryption method that makes zero-knowledge range proofs take up less space. Dero also has built-in atomic exchanges that let people trade one coin for another without using a central exchange. Dero gives people a quick, safe, and cheap way to send and receive funds. Dero has a number of benefits over traditional fiat currencies. For one thing, it is decentralised, which means that it is not controlled by a single group.

This makes it less likely to be affected by inflation because no one can print more Dero. Because they are done on the Dero blockchain, transfers are also quick and cheap and give users a lot of privacy because transactions are anonymous and private. Dero is also fungible, which means that each Dero coin can be swapped for another.

What Makes Dero Unique?

Dero was made to improve reliability, privacy, security and usability for millions of users. It used a "build-it-and-they-will-come" strategy, which means that the team first focused on making technology that worked before thinking about how to market it.

To learn more about Dero, go to **www.dero.io**

Key Takeaways

Privacy empowers you to make decisions about what information you want to share and with whom you want to share it. Freedom, security, consent and dignity are all crucial aspects. Privacy isn't about shutting out everyone and everything. It offers safety, control and the ability to grant access. Privacy provides you with the freedom to express yourself, unleash your creativity, and allocate your time and resources as you see fit, without being subjected to the judgement or scrutiny of others.

It safeguards your private moments, your most vulnerable aspirations, your unconventional ideas, and your ability to express your authentic self. Privacy in cryptocurrency transactions is not just a choice, but a crucial aspect for ensuring security, financial confidentiality and personal privacy.

CHAPTER 7

Be The Wise Servant

In order to withstand the storms of life, you have to have a solid foundation (Matthew 7:24-27). That foundation is Jesus Christ. And praise God, we don't have to guess what He wants us to do!

Therefore whosoever heareth these sayings of mine, and doeth them, I will liken him unto a wise man, which built his house upon a rock: And the rain descended, and the floods came, and the winds blew, and beat upon that house; and it fell not: for it was founded upon a rock. And every one that heareth these sayings of mine, and doeth them not, shall be likened unto a foolish man, which built his house upon the sand: And the rain descended, and the floods came, and the winds blew, and beat upon that house; and it fell: and great was the fall of it.

Matthew 7:24-27

He has graciously given us His Word. In order to know what He thinks and what He says about financial breakthrough, you must study the Bible regularly about financial wisdom. But in order to be the wise servant, you must put His word into practice.

Financial planning with privacy cryptocurrency is one of the ways you do this. Remember, it wasn't raining when God told Noah to build the ark. So even if things are good for you now, it doesn't mean the storm isn't coming. If you are serious about wanting to start working toward financial freedom and honouring God with your money, it's going to take a plan. A plan you must put in place so that you can create a private, prosperous and free life outside of the mark of the beast system.

Biblical Message Of Hope Hidden In Bitcoin Block 666,666

A message of hope from the Bible was found in one of the most unusual places possible: a Bitcoin block on the blockchain network of the world's most popular cryptocurrency. Bitcoin blocks are a lasting record of information about transactions on the network. They are like the pages in a book that keeps track of all transactions. But the blocks are also a kind of very hard math puzzle that Bitcoin miners solve with powerful computers in return for BTC tokens, which are a form of payment. On

Monday night, January 18, 2021, a Bible verse was found hidden in the code of BTC block 666,666. A Bible verse from Romans 12:21 was in the message. It said...

Do not be overcome by evil, but overcome evil with good.

Romans 12:21

The message is about the double "666"
number on the block which represents
the number of the mark of the beast. The
Bible says in Revelation 13:18...

Here is wisdom. Let him that hath understanding count
the number of the beast: for it is the number of a man;
and his number is Six hundred threescore and six (666).

                    Revelation 13:18

The Book of Revelation was written by
Saint John the Divine, who had prophetic
dreams about the end of the world and
the Second Coming of Jesus Christ. The
verse (Romans 12:21) will always be a
part of Bitcoin forever. According to the
Bible this means to *live for the good of
others, to be honest with oneself, and
to fight evil with good*. It's a nod to
Bitcoin's main goal, which is to make
money fair and available to everyone.

This great message of hope was added to other important messages in Bitcoin's history, like Satoshi Nakamoto's notes on the genesis block. These words can't be changed, so they stay on the blockchain forever. It was part of Bitcoin's very first transaction, or "genesis" block. It was an article from The Times newspaper about the 2007/2008 financial crisis...

The Times 03/Jan/2009 Chancellor on brink of second bailout for banks.

Satoshi Nakamoto, the mystery person who created Bitcoin, coded that message into the Bitcoin genesis block.

What Does This Mean?

In times of uncertainty and fear, remember that humanity has faced many challenges throughout history and has

always found ways to overcome them.
We have the capacity for resilience,
creativity and compassion and we can
work together to build a better future.
By focusing on our shared values and
working towards common goals, we can
create a world that is more just, peaceful
and sustainable. Remember that hope is
not just a feeling, but an action. Let us
take action towards a brighter future,
and together, we can overcome any
obstacle.

Embrace Hope, Embody Love And Shine Your Light

In times when darkness seems to
prevail, hold onto hope as a guiding
light. Remember that the Antichrist
embodies the personification of evil and
deception, but it also serves as a

reminder of the eternal struggle between good and evil. Amidst the shadows cast by the Antichrist, let us find solace in the unwavering strength of humanity's spirit. For throughout history, we have faced immense challenges and emerged stronger than ever before. The forces of light, love and compassion have always found a way to overcome darkness.

In the face of deception, let truth be your armour. Embrace the power of knowledge, critical thinking, and discernment. Seek understanding and wisdom, for they are potent tools against the charm of falsehood. Remember that unity is our greatest strength. By coming together, transcending differences and embracing our shared humanity, we create a collective shield that no evil can penetrate. Love and empathy have the power to heal wounds, bridge divides and dispel hatred. Have faith in God and in the resilience of the human spirit. Even in the bleakest of times, hope flickers like a candle in the wind, reminding us of our inherent capacity for good.

Let that flame burn bright within you, igniting the hearts of others and sparking a ripple effect of positive change. Lastly, trust in the ultimate triumph of good over evil. The forces of darkness may test your resolve, but they cannot extinguish the indomitable spirit of hope. Hold steadfast to your beliefs, stand firm in your values and know that, together, you can overcome any adversity. The Antichrist is but a fleeting shadow in the grand tapestry of existence. Embrace hope, embody love and shine your light in the face of darkness. Remember, it is through our collective actions and unwavering faith in God and in goodness that we shall prevail. Amen.

Key Takeaways

The solid foundation to withstand the storms of life is Jesus Christ. For you to know what He thinks and what He says about financial breakthrough, you must study the Bible regularly about financial wisdom and put His word into practice. Financial planning with privacy cryptocurrency is one of the ways you do this. We have the capacity for resilience, creativity and compassion and we can work together to build a better future. By focusing on our shared values and working towards common goals, we can create a world that is more just, peaceful and sustainable. Have faith in God and in the resilience of the human spirit.

CHAPTER 8

Rising Above Adversity And Overcoming Challenges With Resilience

Bouncing back from adversity and
growing stronger in your faith

Life is filled with challenges, and as Christians, we are not exempt from facing challenging circumstances. However, we have a unique advantage— the power of faith and the teachings of the Bible. The Bible has given us strategies of how we can overcome challenges with resilience as Christians, principles and practices that strengthens our faith, sustain our hope and empower us to face adversity with courage.

The Source of Your Resilience

Resilience is not merely a product of your own strength and determination; it stems from your relationship with God. You draw your resilience from your faith in Him, knowing that He is your ultimate source of strength. By placing your trust in God, you tap into His infinite power and find comfort in His unwavering love and guidance.

Have not I commanded thee? Be strong and of a good courage; be not afraid, neither be thou dismayed: for the Lord thy God is with thee whithersoever thou goest.

Joshua 1:9

Anchored In God's Word

The Bible is your guidebook for life, and it offers wisdom and encouragement in the face of challenges. By immersing yourself in God's Word, you gain a solid foundation and a renewed perspective. You discover promises of God's faithfulness, instructions for navigating trials and stories of individuals who triumphed through adversity.

Regular study and meditation on Scripture enable you to find strength and hope amidst the storms of life.

For the word of God is quick, and powerful, and sharper than any twoedged sword, piercing even to the dividing asunder of soul and spirit, and of the joints and marrow, and is a discerner of the thoughts and intents of the heart.

Hebrews 4:12

Prayer: Your Lifeline To God

Prayer is a powerful tool that connects you to your Heavenly Father. It is through prayer that you express your needs, fears and desires to God. In challenging times, you can find solace and strength by pouring out your heart to Him. Prayer cultivates intimacy with God, allowing you to experience His peace that surpasses understanding.

Through prayer, you align your will with His and receive guidance and strength to persevere.

Rejoice evermore.
Pray without ceasing.
In every thing give thanks: for this is the will of God in Christ Jesus concerning you.

1 Thessalonians 5:16-18

Trusting God's Sovereignty

A vital aspect of resilience as a Christian is trusting in God's sovereignty. You must recognize that He is in control of all things, even in the midst of trials that will come during the end times. Trusting God's sovereignty means surrendering your circumstances to Him, acknowledging that His plans are greater than yours. It requires embracing the truth that He can use your challenges for your growth and His glory.

Trust in the Lord with all thine heart; and lean not unto thine own understanding. In all thy ways acknowledge him, and he shall direct thy paths.

Proverbs 3:5-6

Community Support

You were not meant to face challenges alone. God designed us for community, and it is within the fellowship of believers that you find support and encouragement. Surrounding yourself with fellow Christians who can pray for you, provide guidance and offer practical assistance strengthens your resilience. We are called to bear one another's burdens and uplift each other in challenging times.

And let us consider one another to provoke unto love and to good works: Not forsaking the assembling of ourselves together, as the manner of some is; but exhorting one another: and so much the more, as ye see the day approaching.

Hebrews 10:24-25

Cultivating A Christ-Centered Mindset

Resilience begins in the mind. As Christians, we are called to renew our minds and align our thoughts with God's truth. By intentionally focusing on His promises, you can combat negative thinking, fear and doubt. A Christ-centered mindset acknowledges that challenges are temporary, and that God's power is at work in your life. You can reframe your challenges as opportunities for growth and as platforms to testify to God's faithfulness.

Embracing God's Strength In Your Weakness

In your moment of weakness, you have a unique opportunity to experience God's strength. Apostle Paul reminds us that when we are weak, then we are strong, for it is in our weakness that God's power is made perfect (2 Corinthians 12:10). Rather than relying on your own abilities, you surrender to God and allow Him to work through you. This surrender brings forth resilience, knowing that God's grace is sufficient for you in every circumstance.

Perseverance In Faith

Resilience requires perseverance. As Christians, we are called to run the race with endurance, knowing that victory awaits us. In the face of challenges, you press forward, holding onto your faith and refusing to give up. We draw inspiration from the examples of Biblical figures who endured hardships and emerged victorious. By persevering in faith, you grow in resilience and become a living testimony of God's grace. One Bible story that exemplifies perseverance in faith is the story of Job.

Job was a wealthy and righteous man who faced severe trials and tribulations, including the loss of his wealth, his children and his own health. Despite these tremendous adversities, Job remained steadfast in his faith and did not waver in his trust in God. Throughout the Book of Job, Job expresses his anguish and questions why he is suffering. Despite his confusion and despair, Job never curses God or turns away from Him. Instead, he perseveres in his faith and continues to seek God's understanding and wisdom. One verse that captures Job's perseverance in faith is Job 13:15, which says...

Though he slay me, yet will I trust in him: but I will maintain mine own ways before him.

This verse demonstrates Job's unwavering commitment to trust in God, even in the face of great adversity. It reflects his determination to hold on to his faith and maintain his integrity, regardless of the circumstances. The story of Job serves as a powerful reminder that perseverance in faith involves staying steadfast even when life becomes overwhelmingly challenging. It teaches us to trust in God's sovereignty and to remain faithful, even when you do not understand the reasons behind your challenges.

Finding Purpose In Challenges

Challenges can serve as opportunities for spiritual growth and refinement. You can find purpose in your challenges by seeking God's guidance and discerning the lessons He wants to teach you. You can develop empathy and compassion as you identify with the suffering of others.

By embracing your challenges with faith and resilience, you become a vessel through which God's redemptive work can shine. Your resilience in the face of challenges is rooted in your faith in God. By anchoring yourself in His Word, relying on prayer, trusting in His sovereignty, and drawing support from your Christian community, you can overcome any obstacle that comes your way.

Resilience is not a product of your own strength alone but is a testament to the transforming power of your faith in Jesus Christ. As you persevere and find purpose in your challenges, you bring glory to God and inspire others to face their own trials with unwavering hope and resilience.

Focus On The Prize

It is essential for you to focus on the prize set before you. Your ultimate prize is **eternal life** and **communion with God** that awaits you in heaven. As you navigate through the ups and downs of life, it is crucial to maintain an eternal perspective. The Bible reminds us that

our time on earth is temporary, and our
true citizenship is in heaven...

For our conversation is in heaven; from whence also we
look for the Saviour, the Lord Jesus Christ.

Philippians 3:20

By focusing on the prize of eternal life,
you gain a broader perspective that
helps you prioritize what truly matters.

Fixing Your Gaze On Jesus

Jesus Christ is the centrepiece of our
faith, and fixing your gaze on Him
enables you to stay focused on the prize.
He is the author and perfecter of our
faith (Hebrews 12:2), and His life and
teachings provide us with a model to
follow.

Looking unto Jesus the author and finisher of our faith;
who for the joy that was set before him endured the cross,

despising the shame, and is set down at the right hand of
the throne of God.

Hebrews 12:2

By keeping your eyes on Jesus, you are reminded of His sacrificial love, His example of humility and obedience, and the hope He offers through His resurrection.

Embracing Kingdom Values

Focusing on the prize involves aligning your life with the values of God's kingdom. Jesus taught us to seek first the kingdom of God and His righteousness...

But seek ye first the kingdom of God, and his righteousness; and all these things shall be added unto you.

Matthew 6:33

By prioritizing spiritual growth, pursuing righteousness, practicing love and forgiveness, and serving others, you actively participate in the unfolding of God's kingdom on earth. Your focus on the prize helps you make choices that reflect your commitment to God's eternal purposes.

Overcoming Distractions

In a world filled with distractions, it is easy to lose sight of the prize. Material possessions, worldly ambitions and the pursuit of temporary pleasures can divert your attention from what truly matters. Recognizing these distractions and intentionally guarding your heart and mind against them is crucial in maintaining your focus on the eternal prize.

Enduring Through Trials

Focusing on the prize empowers you to endure through trials and adversities. Apostle Paul compares the challenges we face to a race, urging us to run with perseverance and keep our eyes fixed on the goal...

Wherefore seeing we also are compassed about with so great a cloud of witnesses, let us lay aside every weight, and the sin which doth so easily beset us, and let us run with patience the race that is set before us, Looking unto Jesus the author and finisher of our faith; who for the joy that was set before him endured the cross, despising the shame, and is set down at the right hand of the throne of God.

Hebrews 12:1-2

When you encounter challenges, your hope in the eternal prize gives you the strength to press on, knowing that your

present sufferings are temporary
compared to the glory that awaits you.

Seeking Heavenly Treasures

Jesus taught us to store up treasures in
heaven rather than on earth...

Lay not up for yourselves treasures upon earth, where
moth and rust doth corrupt, and where thieves break
through and steal: But lay up for yourselves treasures in
heaven, where neither moth nor rust doth corrupt, and
where thieves do not break through nor steal: For where
your treasure is, there will your heart be also.

Matthew 6:19-21

Focusing on the prize reminds you that
your ultimate reward is found in God's
presence and the eternal blessings He
has prepared for you. This mindset
encourages you to invest your time,
talents and resources in endeavours that
have eternal significance, such as

sharing the gospel, serving others and living lives of righteousness and holiness.

Spreading The Good News

Keeping our eyes on the prize motivates us to share the good news of Jesus Christ with others. Our desire for others to experience the same hope and eternal life compels us to proclaim the gospel boldly. You become a witness to the transformative power of Jesus, offering people the opportunity to join you in pursuing the ultimate prize.

Focusing on the prize is not a mere abstract concept, but a powerful motivator that shapes your beliefs, attitudes and actions. By fixing your gaze on Jesus, embracing an eternal perspective and prioritizing the values of God's kingdom, you can navigate life's challenges with hope and perseverance.

Your ultimate prize of eternal life with God shapes your priorities, helps you overcome distractions and inspires you to live life that honour and glorify Him. May you continually fix your eyes on the prize, running the race of faith with endurance, and encouraging others to join you in the pursuit of the eternal reward that awaits you in Heaven.

Key Takeaways

As Christians we have a unique advantage—the power of faith and the teachings of the Bible. The Bible has given us strategies of how we can overcome challenges with resilience, principles and practices that strengthens our faith, sustain our hope and empower us to face adversity with courage.

Trust in God's sovereignty and recognize that He is in control of all things, even in the midst of trials that will come during the end times. Trusting God's sovereignty means surrendering your circumstances to Him, acknowledging that His plans are greater than yours. It requires embracing the truth that He can use your challenges for your growth and His glory.

CHAPTER 9
Cultivating A Victorious Spirit

Cultivating a victorious spirit involves developing a mindset and attitude that aligns with the truths and promises of God's Word. As a Christian, your identity is rooted in Christ. You are a child of God, redeemed by the blood of Jesus, and empowered by the Holy Spirit.

Cultivating a victorious spirit begins with understanding and embracing your true identity. We are more than conquerors through Christ who loves us.

Nay, in all these things we are more than conquerors through him that loved us. Romans 8:37

By recognizing your position in Him, you can face challenges with confidence and overcome any obstacle that comes your way.

Renewing Your Mind

Victory starts in the mind. Apostle Paul encourages us to renew our minds and transform our thinking.

And be not conformed to this world: but be ye transformed by the renewing of your mind, that ye may prove what is that good, and acceptable, and perfect, will of God.

Romans 12:2

This involves aligning your thoughts with God's truth and rejecting destructive and defeatist thinking patterns. By filling your mind with Scripture, meditating on God's promises and focusing on positive and uplifting thoughts, you create a foundation for a victorious spirit.

Standing On God's Promises

God's Word is filled with promises of victory and triumph. By studying and meditating on these promises, you can build your faith and cultivate a spirit of victory. Promises such as Jeremiah 29:11, Philippians 4:13 and 1 Corinthians 15:57 remind us that God is with us, He is for us and He has already secured the ultimate victory through Christ's death and resurrection.

For I know the thoughts that I think toward you, saith the Lord, thoughts of peace, and not of evil, to give you an expected end. Jeremiah 29:11

I can do all things through Christ which strengtheneth me.
Philippians 4:13

But thanks be to God, which giveth us the victory through
our Lord Jesus Christ. 1 Corinthians 15:57

Standing on these promises empowers you to face challenges with courage and assurance.

Worship

Worship is a powerful tool in cultivating a victorious spirit. Through worship, you can bring your concerns, needs and challenges to God, seeking His guidance and strength. Worship allows you to magnify God's greatness and shift your focus from your challenges to His power. Engaging in regular worship fosters a deep sense of connection with God and helps you maintain a victorious perspective.

Enter into his gates with thanksgiving, and into his courts with praise: be thankful unto him, and bless his name.

Psalm 100:4

Walking In Faith

Faith is the key to victory. Hebrews 11:1 defines faith as the assurance (substance) of things hoped for and the evidence (conviction) of things not seen.

Now faith is the substance of things hoped for, the evidence of things not seen. Hebrews 11:1

Cultivating a victorious spirit requires actively exercising and growing in faith. This involves trusting God's character and His promises, even when circumstances seem challenging. By walking in faith, you access God's supernatural power and experience His faithfulness in your life.

Overcoming Fear And Doubt

Fear and doubt can hinder your ability to walk in victory. Cultivating a victorious spirit requires confronting and overcoming undesirable emotions. The Bible repeatedly encourages us not to fear and to trust in the Lord...

Fear thou not; for I am with thee: be not dismayed; for I am thy God: I will strengthen thee; yea, I will help thee; yea, I will uphold thee with the right hand of my righteousness. Isaiah 41:10

What time I am afraid, I will trust in thee.

Psalm 56:3

By intentionally surrendering your fears and doubts to God, you can replace them with faith and confidence in His ability to overcome any obstacle. By pressing on in faith, even in the face of adversity, you develop resilience and experience the faithfulness of God. Victory often comes through perseverance and holding onto God's promises. Cultivating a victorious spirit is not about a life free from challenges, but about your mindset, faith and reliance on God's power.

By embracing your identity in Christ, renewing your mind, standing on God's promises, walking in faith, engaging in worship, overcoming fear and doubt and persevering through trials, you can live victoriously. May you strive to cultivate a victorious spirit in all areas of your life, empowered by the truth that you are more than a conqueror in Christ Jesus.

Key Takeaways

As a Christian, your identity is rooted in Christ. You are a child of God, redeemed by the blood of Jesus, and empowered by the Holy Spirit. Cultivating a victorious spirit begins with understanding and embracing your true identity. Victory starts in the mind.

This involves aligning your thoughts with God's truth and rejecting destructive and defeatist thinking patterns. By filling your mind with Scripture, meditating on God's promises and focusing on positive and uplifting thoughts, you create a foundation for a victorious spirit.

CHAPTER 10

Getting Closer To The End-Times

The Second Coming will usher in a world illuminated by the radiant presence of our Saviour, Jesus

We are getting closer and closer to the end-time events that will bring the Church Age to a close, and we know that many people are trying to figure out who the anti-Christ is or will be. But the most important warning we get about the end of the world is that the spirit of lying will be so strong that, if it were possible, even the very elect could be deceived.

For there shall arise false Christs, and false prophets, and shall shew great signs and wonders; insomuch that, if it were possible, they shall deceive the very elect.

Matthew 24:24

How and what will the anti-Christ do to trick and seduce God's chosen people? This has been his plan and strategy since the beginning in the Garden of Eden. When he tried to get rid of the great God of all creation, satan used the word *"I will"*. In other words, he was very proud in his heart and wanted to be just like God.

How art thou fallen from heaven, O Lucifer, son of the morning! How art thou cut down to the ground, which didst weaken the nations! For thou hast said in thine heart, I will ascend into heaven, I will exalt my throne above the stars of God: I will sit also upon the mount of the congregation, in the sides of the north: I will ascend above the heights of the clouds; I will be like the most High. Yet thou shalt be brought down to hell, to the sides of the pit.

Isaiah 14:12-15

How can you protect yourself from the strong lies of the end times? Simply put, the degree to which we have pride in our hearts is the degree to which we can be tricked, and it's easy to tell how proud we are by how often we use the word *"I"* in our speech. Pride is what satan gives us instead of God's love and worth, which are unlimited. God made every man and woman to feel like they are important and valuable. But where do we go when we feel nervous, afraid or jealous of someone else?

Satan is all about being proud, while Christ is all about being humble. Pride is the trickiest trap you can fall into. First, because everyone does it and it's so normal, we almost always dislike it. Second, this world recognises people who can boast in a sneaky way about who they are and what they have. No, we won't take pride that's in your face, but we almost always accept pride that's hidden. God's Word tells us to learn about Jesus. What are we supposed to learn about Him?

Come unto me, all ye that labour and are heavy laden, and I will give you rest. Take my yoke upon you, and learn of me; for I am meek and lowly in heart: and ye shall find rest unto your souls. For my yoke is easy, and my burden is light.

Matthew 11:28-30

But made himself of no reputation, and took upon him the form of a servant, and was made in the likeness of men: And being found in fashion as a man, he humbled himself, and became obedient unto death, even the death of the cross.

Philippians 2:7-8

As a child of God, are you meant to ever boast? Yes, surprisingly the Bible has a lot of verses where you can boast. For example, the Apostle Paul says, *"I glory in"*. *"I glory in"* when translated does mean *"to boast about"*. But you never boast about *yourself*, but about who God is and what He has done for you.

In Romans 5:3, Paul says that he is proud of his tribulations (sufferings) and challenges. Paul's biggest wish was to be *"like Christ"*, and as a Christian you go through challenging times so that you can become more like God, your great saviour.

And not only so, but we glory in tribulations also: knowing that tribulation worketh patience; And patience, experience; and experience, hope: And hope maketh not ashamed; because the love of God is shed abroad in our hearts by the Holy Ghost which is given unto us.

Romans 5:3-5

I know you would never think to *"boast"* about your sufferings. What would happen if you change your mind and decide to *"rejoice"* in every challenging situation? If you do, you would have a lot less worry because the enemy would not like it if you use every situation as a chance to talk about how great your God is. By doing that, God hears about your prayers to make you more like Jesus by letting you go through situations that teaches you to be strong, patient, hopeful and expectant.

The Bible says in James 1:2-5...

My brethren, count it all joy when ye fall into divers temptations; Knowing this, that the trying of your faith worketh patience. But let patience have her perfect work, that ye may be perfect and entire, wanting nothing. If any of you lack wisdom, let him ask of God, that giveth to all men liberally, and upbraideth not; and it shall be given him.

James 1:2-5

May the Lord give you the wisdom to know when you boast about something other than how much you love Him. You will be less likely to be misled by lies the more you train yourself to walk in humility. In the last days, you will be easily deceived if you boast about yourself and what you have done. May the Lord free you from the idea that you have to *"boast"* about yourself to show that you are important.

When you boast about something other than God's love, your sense of self-worth is broken. We don't usually realise this and get stuck in a circle of boasting that does the opposite of what we think it will. Pride is satan's imitation of God's unending love, which has given you a lot of worth because He gave up His own Son to pay for your salvation. Let that be your constant claim, and you won't be deceived in the end times.

Message Of Hope For The Second Coming Of Christ

In a world often plagued by uncertainty and turmoil, the promise of Christ's Second Coming brings forth a message of unwavering hope and profound transformation. It reminds us that amidst the challenges we face, there is a higher purpose, a divine plan unfolding before us.

The Second Coming of Christ signifies the fulfillment of prophecies, the restoration of righteousness, and the ultimate triumph of light over darkness. It is a beacon of hope, assuring us that justice will prevail, and love will reign supreme. In the anticipation of Christ's return, let us find comfort in the profound love and mercy that He embodies. His teachings of compassion, forgiveness, and unity serve as a guiding light, illuminating the path towards a world filled with peace and harmony. Through His Second Coming, we are reminded of the inherent goodness within humanity. It is a call to awaken our spirits, to embrace our divine nature, and to recognize the interconnectedness of all beings.

In this recognition, we can foster compassion and empathy, extending a helping hand to those in need and building a world characterized by unity and understanding. The Second Coming is a catalyst for transformation, both on an individual and collective level. It calls upon us to examine our lives, to shed the burdens of ego and materialism, and to embrace the values of love, kindness, and service. It is an opportunity for spiritual growth and renewal, as we align ourselves with the eternal truths and embrace the divine potential within. Let the promise of the Second Coming inspire us to work towards a world that mirrors the teachings of Jesus Christ. Let us strive to create communities of love and acceptance, where the marginalized are uplifted and the broken are healed.

May we sow seeds of peace, justice, and reconciliation, and cultivate an environment where every soul can flourish and thrive. In the face of adversity, let the hope of Christ's Second Coming be your anchor. It is a reminder that no matter how daunting the challenges, love is more powerful than hatred, and righteousness will ultimately prevail. Hold fast to this hope, nurture it within your heart, and let it guide your actions as we eagerly await the glorious return of our Saviour. The Second Coming of Christ is a testament to the boundless grace and infinite possibilities that await us.

Embrace this hope, let it inspire you to live a life of purpose and meaning, and be a beacon of light in a world yearning for the transformative power of love. Together, as we await the dawn of a new era, let us journey in faith, hope and anticipation, knowing that the Second Coming will usher in a world illuminated by the radiant presence of our Saviour, Jesus.

Key Takeaways

Pride is what satan gives us instead of God's love and worth, which are unlimited. God made every man and woman to feel like they are important and valuable. Satan is all about being proud, while Christ is all about being humble. Pride is the trickiest trap you can fall into. Use every situation as a chance to talk about how great your God is.

By doing that, God hears about your prayers to make you more like Jesus by letting you go through situations that teaches you to be strong, patient, hopeful and expectant. His teachings of compassion, forgiveness and unity serve as a guiding light, illuminating the path towards a world filled with peace and harmony.

You Are Priceless

For what profit is it to a man if he gains the whole world and loses his own soul? Or what will a man give in exchange for his soul? (Matthew 16:26).

No man, as yet, has been able to amass for himself all the wealth of the world – everything; but even if it were possible to have the whole world, it is still not worth it to forfeit your salvation for the world. The salvation of your soul is the most priceless thing. It is the best thing to ever happen in the life of man. All of the world – the wealth of its cities, the value of its facilities, the trillions of money that circulate in the financial market and those held in the vaults of banks, the rich deposits of minerals, fame and luxury, etc. – all added together cannot make up for salvation. The salvation of your soul is not something you can compromise on. For salvation is everlasting just as the soul is eternal. Moreover, humanity has been so blessed in that this valuable salvation is given at no cost; **_you do not pay anything to have salvation._**

How? Why? Because it has been paid for already by one man, Jesus Christ, and the price for salvation was certainly not cheap. *Salvation was paid for in blood. The blood of a perfect, righteous man-God, Jesus Christ.* Jesus Christ, though had all the power to make Him invincible, had to just allow

Himself to be crucified on the cross. Jesus substituted Himself for us, in that He gave us His righteousness and took our unrighteousness because God has a purpose at heart to save you from sin, satan, death (separation from God), hell and eternal condemnation for sin. The salvation call is ongoing; God is still calling you to salvation.

Through the Scriptures, His voice rings out –... *"In the time of my favour I heard you, and in the day of salvation I helped you. I tell you, now is the time of God's favour, now is the day of salvation"*. (2 Corinthians 6:2)

Salvation is a choice. You can make that choice now. In fact, you are a prayer away from your salvation; the

Bible says, *"That if you confess with your mouth, "Jesus is Lord", and believe in your heart that God raised him from the dead, you will be saved. For it is with your heart that you believe and are justified, and it is with your mouth that you confess and are saved".* (Romans 10:9-10). With regard to Romans 10:9-10, if you have heeded the salvation call and you are ready to receive salvation, then say this prayer:

"Lord Jesus, I believe you came to die on the cross for my sins and resurrected on the third day. I repent of my sins and ask for your forgiveness. I accept you as my Lord and Saviour. Amen"

CONGRATULATIONS!

YOU ARE NOW SAVED

Having believed and said such a prayer, be sure of this – Jesus has given you salvation; meaning, you have eternal life, you have been born again and forgiven of all sins committed. It is a spiritual experience; it is the work of God.

Congratulations on heeding the salvation call! You are a born-again Christian now. Well done for sincerely accepting Jesus Christ as your Lord and Saviour. Taking the decision to believe and become a follower of Jesus is your best decision ever; for you will never regret making such a decision.

Amen.

DDD

Other Books By The Author

The Great Revelation: Biblical Strategies Against CBDCs And How To Prosper In The Brave New World

The global banking cartel is hard at work engineering a new form of money that will serve as the backbone of the most sophisticated system of financial surveillance and control the world has ever seen. This financial surveillance system (CBDCs) is to be fully implemented by 2025 across all countries in the world. This could usher in the mark of the beast financial system as prophesised in the Book of Revelation 13.

For a full list of all books by the author, go to...

https://bit.ly/dwase22

Discovering And Enjoying God's Purpose For Your Life

Each individual has been created by God with distinct gifts and talents, each intended to serve a unique purpose. As a Christian, your true purpose and meaning in life stem from utilising your abilities to serve God and further His kingdom. As you deepen your connection with God, He will gradually unveil His plans for your life with greater clarity.

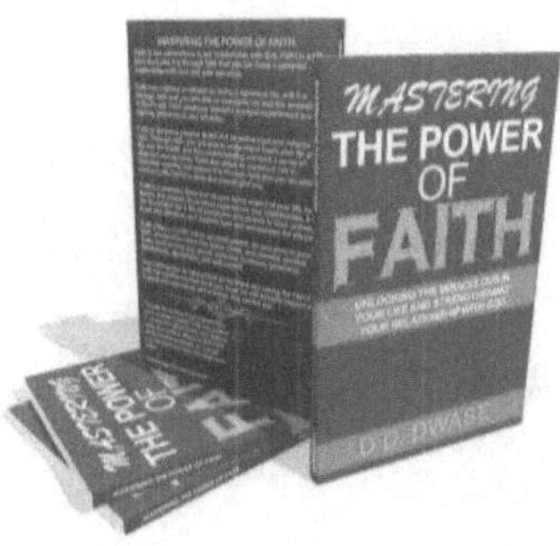

Mastering The Power Of Faith: Unlocking The Miraculous In Your Life And Strengthening Your Relationship With God

Faith is our cornerstone in our relationship with God. Faith is a gift from God, and it is through faith that you can have a personal relationship with God and gain salvation. Faith has a strong emphasis on living a righteous life, and it is through faith that you are able to overcome sin and live according to God's will. Discover how faith produces powerful spiritual experiences such as healing, deliverance, and miracles.

The Great Commandment: Discovering The Heart of Christianity And Embracing The Divine Plan

The *"Great Commandment"* emphasizes the importance of both loving and serving God, and loving and treating others with compassion and kindness. It is the idea of loving God with all your heart, soul, and mind that represents a complete and all-encompassing love and devotion to God, which is the highest form of worship. It means putting God first in all things and seeking to honour and serve Him in every aspect of life. Loving your neighbour as yourself, on the other hand, involves treating others with

kindness, compassion, and respect, just as you
would want to be treated.

Mastering Your Emotions: A Practical Guide To Living A Positive, Fulfilled And Abundant Life

"Mastering Your Emotions" and discovering your true self is possible, and when you choose to be authentic and in integrity with your true self, you will realize that everything falls in place. Life can be so much more when you know who you are and where you are going. When you shift your focus to who you are and what you want out of life, you find your true self.

Mastering The Power of Your Destiny And Purpose-Filled Life: Strategies To Activate Success In Your Life

Every one of us has a special purpose on this planet, and a singular life that belongs to us and us alone. Each of us has a duty to honour the purpose that we were meant to serve, and we are allowed to continue to create the changes that need to be made in order to make those dreams a reality. What most of us are lacking is the basic structure to get to where we want to be. Accomplishing your goals may seem obscure and idealistic, but there are steps that you can take every single day to get to where you want to be.

With this book you will begin to see that it is
not only possible, but how to obtain the power
to turn dreams into reality.

Mastering The Law of Attraction: The Missing Key To Tapping Into The Universe And Manifesting Your Dreams And Desires

According to the Law of Attraction, your thoughts and emotions are responsible for attracting certain things into your life. This means that you can have, do, or become anything you want as long as you use your mind in good ways. The key to a happy and successful life is understanding this universal law. The Law of Attraction may assist you in every facet of your life. Make use of it not only to obtain what you want, but also to grow into the person you want to be. The Law of Attraction is a self-fulfilling prophecy.

According to this law, you will attract into
your life whatever it is that you give the
majority of your attention, energy, and ideas
to.

Mastering The Power of Positive Thinking: How To Attract Success, Happiness And Prosperity Through The Power of Positive Thinking

Imagine your life as a reflection of what you imagine in your mind. Your thoughts are the first step in making positive changes in your life and must be altered if you are to change. Your life and even your environment are influenced by thoughts that are frequently repeated in your subconscious mind. With enough practice, your subconscious mind will believe that they are real and make any changes that are needed to make your real life match your inner fantasies. Thoughts have the power to help you build a new career, change

your relationships, become financially free or
improve your quality of life.

**Mastering Bitcoin For Beginners:
Bitcoin, Cryptocurrency And The
Future Of Money**

Bitcoin is a revolutionary new form of digital currency that operates on a peer-to-peer model rather than a centralized government model. This book covers everything you need to know in order to get started with Bitcoin such as...

- *Understanding Bitcoin*
- *Use Cases of Bitcoin And The Blockchain*
- *How To Buy/Invest in Bitcoin*
- *How To Secure Your Bitcoin*
- *The Best Bitcoin Wallet*
- *Benefits of Bitcoin*

- *How To Use Bitcoin As Inflationary Hedge*
- *A Future With Bitcoin and much more!*

For a full list of all books by the author, go to…

https://bit.ly/dwase22

or scan the QR code below…

ABOUT THE AUTHOR

D.D. Dwase is the founder and Senior Pastor of Vision Chapel. Vision Chapel is a church centered on *"Proclaiming Christ and Winning Souls"* as well as loving God and loving people. He believes in preaching Biblical truths in a practical, relatable way to help his congregation apply God's word to their daily lives. He strives to lead with humility, compassion and wisdom.

His Sunday sermons attract both long-time church members and new visitors seeking meaning and purpose in life. Under his leadership, Vision Chapel has become a thriving church that warmly welcomes people from all walks of life. He has helped expand community outreach programs, youth mentoring and more. He invites anyone seeking a place to belong, grow their faith and make a difference through acts of service to visit Vision Chapel. Outside of his pastoral duties, D.D. Dwase enjoys spending time with his wife, Pastor Josephine and their daughter.

D.D. Dwase feels blessed to serve the Vision Chapel congregation and build a church where inspired worship, Godly teaching and compassionate care come together. He looks forward to many more years of ministry focused on making devoted disciples of Jesus Christ in the pursuit of the eternal reward that awaits us in Heaven.

Visit… www.visionchapel.org

9 798224 945030